Wicca Starter Kit

The Ultimate Beginner's Guide to Wiccan Magic, Spells, Rituals, Essential Oils, and Witchcraft

Dora Rosewood

© **Copyright 2020 Dora Rosewood- All rights reserved.**

The content contained within this book may not be reproduced, duplicated, or transmitted without direct written permission from the author or the publisher.

Under no circumstances will any blame or legal responsibility be held against the publisher, or author, for any damages, reparation, or monetary loss due to the information contained within this book. Either directly or indirectly.

Legal Notice:

This book is copyright protected. This book is only for personal use. You cannot amend, distribute, sell, use, quote or paraphrase any part, or the content within this book, without the consent of the author or publisher.

Disclaimer Notice:

Please note the information contained within this document is for educational and entertainment purposes only. All effort has been executed to present accurate, up to date, and reliable, complete information. No warranties of any kind are declared or implied. Readers acknowledge that the author is not engaging in the rendering of legal, financial, medical, or professional advice. The content within this book has been derived from various sources. Please consult a licensed professional before attempting any techniques outlined in this book.

By reading this document, the reader agrees that under no circumstances is the author responsible for any losses, direct or indirect, which are incurred as a result of the use of information contained within this document, including, but not limited to, — errors, omissions, or inaccuracies.

Table of Contents

Introduction 8

Chapter 1 10

An Introduction to Wicca

- What is Wicca
- What is Magic?
- Goals
- Eight Common Types of Magic
- Wiccan God and Goddess
- The duality of the God
- Wheel of the Year
- Sabbats

Chapter 2 47

The History of Witchcraft in Wicca

- Ancient Inspirations
- Modern Inspirations
- Magical Tools

Chapter 3 66
Wiccan Traditions and Practices

- Popular Wiccan Traditions
    1. Gardnerian
    2. Alexandrian
    3. Dianic
    4. Seax
    5. Norse
    6. Druidic and Celtic
- Forms of Practice
    1. Covens
    2. Circles
    3. Solitary Practitioners
    4. Eclectic Wicca

Chapter 4 84
Candle Magic

- What is Candle Magic
- The Magic of Color
- Color and Astrology
- Enhancing Candle Magic

- Divine Communication Through Candles
- Spells and Rituals Using Candles

Chapter 5 103
Crystal Magic

- What Is Crystal Magi
- Cleansing Your Crystals
- Charging Your Crystals
- Popular Crystals and Their Uses
- Spells and Rituals Using Crystals

Chapter 6 130
Herbal Magic

- What is Herbal Magic
- Learning About Herbs
- Easy to Grow Herbs
- Bath Teas
- Soaps
- Body Powder
- Tea
- Tea Blends

Chapter 7 ....**137**
Divination Magic

- The Tarot

- Major Arcana Card Meanings
- Scrying
- Dowsing

Chapter 8..**162**
Essential Oils

- What are Essential Oils
- How to Make Your Own Essential Oils
- Where to Buy Essential Oils
- Example Oil Blends
- House Fresheners/ Cleaners

Chapter 9..**174**
Empaths and the Highly In-Tuned

Chapter 10..**183**
Popular Terms

Conclusion...**189**

Introduction

The first few chapters will cover the history of Witchcraft in Wicca, basic magical principles both ancient and modern, an introduction to Wicca and the God, Goddess and celebrations, the how and why of magic, Wiccan traditions, circles, and solitary practitioners.

The following chapters will dive into different kinds of magic:

- Candle magic and a few rituals and spells involving them, along with their meanings and associations.
- Crystal magic and how you can infuse your magical intent into them, spells and rituals using them, and how to cleanse them.
- Herbal Magic and the most common herbs, easy herbs to grow yourself, soaps, house cleaner, teas, etc.

We will also discuss essential oils and how to make your own, along with common tools used in spells, rituals, and magical practices.

To end, we will touch on empaths and those who are highly in-tuned to the Divine, giving helpful tips and tricks to both discover if you fall into these categories and how to manage easier if you do.

There are plenty of books on this subject on the market, thanks again for choosing this one! Every effort was made to ensure it is full of as much useful information as possible, please enjoy!

Chapter 1
An Introduction to Wicca

What is Wicca

Wicca is a modern religion rooted in ancient traditions. Followers of the Path typically worship Nature and the Divine, along with practicing Witchcraft. It is referred to by many as the 'Old Religion' because Witchcraft is arguably one of the oldest practices in the world and is a big part of Wicca. It's important to note one can be a Witch without being Wiccan in much the same way that one could be Christian without being Lutheran, though many use the terms interchangeably.

Wicca is considered a Neo-Pagan religion, because although it has many practices that date back thousands of years, Wicca is a fairly new religion only dating back to 20th century Britain. Since Nature and the Divine are such big aspects of Wicca, the goal of practitioners is to connect and understand the Divine as the beginning and end of all Nature's mysteries.

They generally worship the Goddess and the God, though certain traditions only acknowledge the Goddess. They use their energy and the energy of the

Universe around them to work magic, cast spells, and honor their Deities.

Most of the Wiccan way of life and belief systems are based on reconstructed pre-Christian traditions from Wales, Scotland, and Ireland. They're reconstructed for the simple fact a majority of the information that existed, was eradicated by the Medieval church in their efforts to erase Pagan traditions from history.

Wiccans practice acceptance and tolerance to other religions, even acknowledging their path isn't the only way to achieving spirituality, so long as those faiths don't violate their tenant of 'Harm None.' For this reason, there are Christian Wiccans, Buddhist Wiccans, Jewish Wiccans – the list can be practically endless.

What is Magic?

The word 'magic' comes from the French word 'magique,' which was adopted in the late 1300S. The French definition was to produce marvels and influence events using natural forces that were hidden. For Wiccans, when it first began, it was simply described as sending thoughts to manifest in the spiritual plane and come back to the physical plane. Now, though, to the 21st-century Witch, the definition is to participate consciously in the co-creative Universal forces by directing energy in Nature to change one's life based on their desires.

Magic, in simple terms, is simply utilizing the power of thought and expressing it to the Universe and the Divine in a way that helps it manifest and become true and able to make a change in your life. It is commonly referred to as Witchcraft or the Craft to convey the amount of skill involved in mastering it.

So, like any skill, practice makes perfect. And though there are certainly natural witches – meaning they were born with the gift – those who wish to be successful in their spellcasting and magical workings need to practice! Being patient and checking yourself when you feel self-doubt or skepticism creeping up on you is so important. Most times, if your magic isn't working, it's because you believe it won't before you even start.

You may have seen the spelling 'magick' and wondered if there was a difference. It's really all down to personal preference and which spelling you connect with. Alastair Crowley coined the change in spelling, adding the 'k' to differentiate between the magic stage magicians and illusionists practiced versus the religious sort.

Goals

There are common goals all Witches and practitioners of magic strive to achieve, and they are generally directed at bettering one's circumstance:

- Protection
- Love
- Wealth
- Physical well-being

Many also work magic for others betterment and spiritual development. The important thing to remember when doing magic of any kind is to follow one of the most important rules in the Wiccan Rede: "and harm ye none, do what ye will." Magical faith of any kind shouldn't be used to cause harm, whether it be to other human beings or any other living being.

This is important because the Three-Fold Law is a belief firmly held by most Wiccans: "and ever mind the rule of three, what ye send out comes back to thee." All this means is if you work white (good) magic, it will return to you threefold, but the same can be said for working black (dark) magic. In simple words, magic is like a boomerang, so prepare for anything you send out into the Universe to come right back to you. Because of this, many Witches choose to make the distinction between white and black magic by:

- Making their intent clear
- Adding some form of "with harm to none" at the end of their spell
- Performing some form of divination before casting a spell
- Things like scrying or Tarot can be used to see potential outcomes

Eight Common Types of Magic

There are various different forms of magic, but like with all things, there are those that are more common than others.

It's also important to note magic is such a personal art, meaning the practice one Witch uses might not work for you – and that's okay! It's up to each Witch to find the right mix of magic she connects with.

- **High Magic**

High Magic is typically practiced when a Witch or Witches want to influence higher purposes or grow spiritually. It's a very powerful, ritualized magic that requires lots of studies to be mastered. High Magic involves intricate numerology and astrology, symbolism, and calling upon otherworldly entities.

- **Low Magic or Earth Magic**

Low Magic is typically concerned with everyday life – the more mundane nuances often targeted in spellwork

– safe travels, love, etc. – and is typically less ceremonial than High Magic. As with all forms of magic, practices is never a bad thing, but Low Magic relies more heavily on spontaneity, instinct, and creativity.

It is important to note the terms High and Low do not denote status. One type of magic is not superior to the other; they are simply different.

- **Divination**

Many forms of magic fall under the category of divination – anything that uses seeing into the future in search of answers. We will discuss some of these in more detail in the later chapters, but a few forms of divination are:

- **Tarot**

The first deck of Tarot cards was made in Italy in the 1500S

Contains 78 cards

Major Arcana is the most powerful

Specific cards can be incorporated into spells Moon card during full Moon Spell

King/ Queen of Pentacles for prosperity spells Some Witches choose to do a Tarot reading before creating a spell

Can take several years to master

- **Runes**

First known writing system Developed by Germanic peoples Each represents the impressive force

Scrying

Using a pendulum, mirror, dark glass bowl, etc. in order to see visions and receive answers

- **Tea leaves**

Used to see upcoming events Years of practice Interpretation involved

Looking for signs/ shapes/ visions within the leave

- **Sympathetic Magic**

Sympathetic magic, simply put, involves using an object to represent someone so that the two become joined together. After this magical working has been completed, what happens to the object then happens to the person it is tied to.

Many people have heard of this form of magic through the use of Voodoo dolls, but it is important to note this magic isn't always used negatively. Many use it for love, healing, and prosperity.

- **Talismanic Magic**

This, much like divination magic, can have a bit of a broad spectrum. Simply put, this is any kind of magic used to create an amulet or talisman. These are items – crystals, stones, necklaces, sprigs of herbs, etc. – that have been charmed for a particular purpose like for love, protection, or repelling/ drawing energies and are then worn.

- **Folk Magic**

Folk magic is a very practical form of magic that can be attributed back to cultures and families since before the origins were traceable. It is often seen as one of the most spontaneous and least ritualized forms of magic involving natural items, gestures, chants, and symbols.

A practical example of this is placing a hex sign on a door to keep evil at bay.

- **Elemental Magic**

This form of magic, like divination, entails many different forms of magic that will be discussed more fully in their own chapters. The basis of Elemental Magic is invoking the Four Sacred Elements – Earth, Air, Fire, and Water.

Each element corresponds to a direction, color, and magical tool, and all of these need to be considered when practicing Elemental Magic because it can be a very powerful force. The different forms of Elemental Magic are:

- Planetary
- Moon
- Rune
- Color
- Musical
- Kitchen
- Herbal
- Candle

- Crystal
- Metal
- Tarot

- **Petition Magic**

This magic is the closest to resembling prayer and is used to request a Higher Power to award you with what you desire. The important thing to remember is when using Petition Magic, you have to be able to accept 'no' as an answer because sometimes that's the case. You are simply asking for your will to be done.

This form of magic is typically used when one isn't sure whether they have the authority or right to manipulate a situation, but still feel they should make an appeal.

In this way, one is simply giving the issue up to a Higher Being.

- **Wiccan God and Goddess**

Most Wiccan traditions believe in a God and Goddess who created all things. They are viewed as perfect counterparts to the other and are complete equals. She is the Lady to his Lord just as He is the Sun God to Her Moon Goddess. Depending on which tradition you follow; they can be represented by many Deities that you feel a personal connection with, They can simply be archetypes, or each Deity (Hecate, Athena, Dionysus, etc.) are all just different sides of the same All-Powerful.

- **The Triple Goddess**

The Goddess has three aspects: the Maiden, the Mother, and the Crone, and each represents a different phase of a woman's life, the many facets of the human psyche, the cycles of life and death, and different phases of the moon. Because of this three-fold form, she is often known as the Triple Goddess.

The notion of a triple Deity can be traced back to ancient civilizations:

- Greek Goddess Hera

She had three varying roles in mythology:
Girl, Woman, and Widow

- Celtic Goddess Brighid

She ruled over three skills that were crucial in Celtic society: poetry, healing, and smithcraft

It is likely these older Goddesses partly inspired the book The White Goddess: *A Historical Grammar of Poetic Myth* by Robert Graves. This book was important in Wicca's developmental history, though it wasn't until the 1970S that the Triple Goddess as we know her (Maiden, Mother, Crone) was developed.

The Maiden

This aspect of the Goddess is Her youth. She is often shown as the waxing crescent because She represents growth, and the waxing moon 'grows,' transitioning to the full moon. The Maiden also represents new potential and life, beauty, self-confidence, independence, intelligence, creativity and self-expression, exploration, and discovery.

Much like in our own lives, we seek these things in our youth, many of us choosing to travel and broaden our horizons, others flourishing in our self-confidence and new-found independence, and some finding the peak of their creativity. The Maiden can be seen as a young adult, just starting Her true journey.

In Nature She is associated with:

- Spring
- The sunrise
- The dawn

Those who choose to assign a specific Deity to the Maiden typically worship Her in the following forms:

Nordic Goddess Freya Celtic Goddess Rhiannon Greek Goddess Persephone Greek Goddess Artemis

The Mother

The Mother is often thought of as the most powerful aspect of the Goddess because she gave birth to all the abundance of the Earth. Because of this, she is usually represented by the full moon, because in this phase, She has become pregnant by God.

She, like most mothers, represent adulthood, nurturing, life's fullness, and responsibility. She is greatly associated with manifestation, partly due to the belief She is the most powerful. When performing rituals, particularly Calling Down the Moon, she is the aspect that's visualized.

In Nature She is associated with:

- Midday
- Summer
- The Moon

Those who choose to assign a specific Deity to Her generally worship:

- Celtic Goddess Danu
- Celtic Goddess Badb
- Greek Goddess Demeter
- Greek Goddess Selene
- Roman Goddess Ceres

The Crone

The Crone is the older, more wise aspect of the Goddess. This is Her form after having given birth to the new God. In much earlier interpretations of the Triple Goddess, she was referred to as 'the hag.' She is there to remind us that death is part of the cycle of life, and even though She is often feared, she is an integral part of the Universe.

She oversees past lives, death, and rebirth, transformations, prophecy, endings, aging, guidance, and visions. She is also represented by the waning crescent moon because She represents the ending of a cycle, much like the waning crescent represents the ending of the lunar cycle.

In Nature she is associated with:

- Autumn
- Winter
- Sunset
- Night
- The ending of the growing season for crops

Those who choose to assign a specific Deity to the Crone typically worship:

- Celtic Goddess Morrigan
- Celtic Goddess Cailleach Bear
- Russian Baba Yaga
- Greek Goddess Hecate

The Triple God

The God's names are less well-known, therefore a lot of it depends on your tradition and what feels right to you. The most common aspects of God are the Young Lord, the Father, and the Wise Man. He is the Goddess' consort and protector. He is often seen as being associated with hunting, nature, sexuality, and the animal realm.

The Youmg Lord

He is the youngest aspect of God and is known by a few different names:

- The Young God
- The Lord of the Forest
- The Hunter
- The Horned God

He is a young hunter and wanderer, filled with arrogance and great pride. Like most young men, He is learning self-discovery, is at His most sexual, and 'sowing His wild oats'. In this phase, He hasn't yet noticed the Goddess.

Those who choose to assign a specific Deity, typically worship:
- Greek God Pan
- Celtic God Cernunnos
- Greek God Eros
- British Folklore Herne
- Occasionally Gods of War

In Nature He is associated with:
- Dawn
- Sun-up

The Father

The Father is the mature aspect of the God. Depending on which tradition you follow, He is known by the following names:
- The Green Man

- Lord of the Hunt
- Oak King
- The Sun God

This is the aspect that marries the Goddess and becomes a father. He has turned His arrogance to self-confidence and becomes the Goddess' protector and consort.

He rules over all the fields and animals. He is the aspect that is manifested most often, particularly when farmers want their crops to flourish. He is considered the strongest aspect of the God and is full of vitality.

Those who choose to associate a specific Deity to this aspect typically worship:

- Babylonian God Bel
- Greek God Apollo
- Ancient Sun God Mithra
- Nordic God Thor

In Nature He is associated with:

- Waxing Sun
- Animals Forests

The Wise Mam

This aspect of the God is the oldest aspect. Depending on the tradition, he is known by the following names:

- The Sage
- The Oak King
- The Hermit
- The Old Man
- The Magician
- Grandfather of the World
- The Old Man in the Mountain

Here he is coming to the end of his cycle, preparing to join the Crone in the Underworld and await his rebirth as the Young Lord again. He, like many older men, is associated with being calm and wise. He has long since fought and protected his wife and Goddess, and he is now at the winding-down phase of his life. He is seen as a magician, philosopher, and thinker, typically depicted as an old man with a long white beard reading.

Those who choose to assign a specific Deity to this aspect typically worship:

- Nordic God Odin
- Welsh God Owain ab Urien

- Egyptian God Horus
- Egyptian God Thoth

The duality of the God

The first drawing of a Horned Deity was created during the Paleolithic period in the caverns des Trois Freres in Ariege. Drawings and depictions of Horned Deities were also common in Egypt, Mesopotamia, and Babylonia.

Some practitioners, typically Celtic-based, choose to believe in a duality aspect instead of the Triple God. In the image of the Horned God, it is believed that each horn represents a different aspect: the Oak King and the Holly King.

They are two sides of the same coin, representing the changing of seasons from spring and summer to fall and winter. Without one, the other wouldn't exist.

As with most Deities, there is a story behind these two aspects. It is believed there is a battle raging between the Holly King and the Oak King as they fight for supremacy to rule during the Wheel of the Year and battle for the Goddess' favor.

The Oak King

Those who believe in the duality of the God, believe the Oak King kills the Holly King during the Winter Solstice and rules until Midsummer (Litha). He is often viewed as the Lord of the Forest, Green Man, or God of Fertility.

The Holly King

The Holly King takes control at the Summer Solstice, defeating the old Oak King and ruling until the Winter Solstice (Yule, when the God is born).

The Holly King is often depicted as a forestry version of Santa.

He dresses in red with holly in his tangled hair. He is often shown leading a team of eight stags.

Wheel of the Year

The holidays Wiccans observe are referred to as High Holy Days or the sabbats and Esbats. These are all contained within the Wheel of the Year, marking the changing of seasons and phases of life. Each turning of seasons presents a new reason to give thanks and commune with Deity, Universe, and Nature.

Sabbats

The Sabbats occur approximately every 6 weeks, denoting the different life phases and the change of seasons. These are usually celebrated with large groups of family and friends, with lots of drink, food, and rituals, but with the rise in popularity of solitary practitioners, it's no longer uncommon for Witches to celebrate on their own.

Sabbats honor the Sun, which is a representation of the God, so rituals are done on Sabbats usually occur at high-noon, and the celebrations are primarily called Sun Festivals. There are certain traditions that also choose to honor an aspect of Goddess as well, though she is represented by the Moon.

Samhain – October 3Jst

This holiday is also known as Halloween, Feast of the Dead, Feast of Apples, New Year, Festival of Remembrance, All Hallows Eve, and All Souls Night. This is the beginning of the new year.

This is considered the end of the year and denotes the ending of one cycle in preparation for another. It's a time for contemplation and preparation for the upcoming year along with looking back on the year that's passed and honoring those who are no longer here. It is believed the veil between our world and the next is at its thinnest, making communing with friends and family who have passed easier than any other day of the year.

Samhain also marks the last of the year's harvest and was seen as the last time family and friends would be able to gather before settling in for winter. There are a few traditions that occur throughout the different variations of Wicca:

Honoring ancestors

This doesn't have to be complicated.

- Place a photo of family or friends who have passed on your altar and welcome them into your home.
- If you choose to have a feast, as most do, set an extra plate for them, eat some of their favorites, and talk about them.
- For pets, you may want to leave dog food outside in offering – many animals appreciate this treat!

- Walking in Nature
- Performing magic/ ritual by bonfires

- Invoke the Divine in their forms associated with Samhain
    1. Crone Goddess
    2. Horned God
- Hold a séance
    1. Since the veil is thinnest this night, many choose to commune with passed loved ones.
- Make an altar for Samhain or for your ancestors.
- Guiding spirits to the Spirit World
    2. Light a white candle that will burn for 7 days and place it in your window
- Group rituals

The following are popular symbols of Samhain:

- Cauldron

Infinite container for rebirth, death, life, and transformation

- Besom (broom)

Used symbolically and practically to 'sweep out' the old, cleaning not only literal dirt, but old energy as well

- Acorn

The seed of Oak trees

Represent rebirth, wisdom, strength to come, and longevity

Token of good fortune

Yule – Witmer Solstice (~December 2Jst)

This holiday is considered the start of the new year and occurs on the winter solstice (around December 21st). It's a time to solidify plans for the upcoming spring and is considered a fertility celebration because life is beginning to stir after the long winter. Those who believe in the Holly King and Oak King recognize this holiday as the Oak King/ Sun God killing the Holly King and regaining control for the warmer months as the days become longer. Those who believe in the Triple God see this as His rebirth.

The following are common traditions:
- Hanging evergreens

Hung around windows and doorways for everlasting life
- Mistletoe

Viewed as a protector and healer
- Holly

Used to ward off undesirable spirits

- Ivy

Used as a representation of resurrection and reincarnation along with rebirth

- The wreath

Traditionally made to represent the Wheel of Life

Hung on doors

Became Christian Advent Wreath

- Yule Tree

Pine and fir revered as a representation of life and rebirth in the heart of winter

- Giving gifts

This is the God's birthday

Exchanging gifts has been part of Yule since ancient times

Imbolc/ Candlemas (~ January 3Jst/ February 2md)

This holiday marks the first fertility festival of spring, though its date depends on one's specific tradition, but it is usually celebrated between January 31st and February 2nd. Imbolc celebrates renewal and is considered an auspicious time for marriage and blossoming relationships.

Celebrators focus on making way for new things while clearing out the old – much like spring cleaning.

Imbolc also honors the Maiden, the youngest form of the Goddess, and any other Deity who represents love and fertility one feels a closeness to. Traditionally Imbolc honored Brighid, the Goddess of poetry, smithcraft, and healing; the Goddess of Sun, Hearth, and Fire. She is one of the oldest forms of the Triple Goddess and was so loved she became known as St. Bridget in the Christian church.

The following traditions are common during Imbolc:
Making a Brigid Cross

- Making a Brigid doll

You can fill this doll with a wish or special crystal, flowers or special herbs.

- Planting seeds

Each seed you plant can be a representation of your ideas and hopes because they contain pure potential.

- Lighting candles

This is simple magic, allowing you to make wishes for friends and family

Allow candle to burn down completely Never leave a lit candle unattended

Ostara – Spring Equinox (~ March 2Jst)

Ostara is also known as the spring or vernal equinox occurring between the 21st and 22nd of March. This is the time where day and light are in perfect harmony – everything is in balance.

This holiday happens on the day of the spring equinox, which typically falls around the 1st of March. This is a time for planting crops for the new year, so the Gods are invoked for luck with the upcoming crops. Ostara is the second fertility festival of the year out of three, and many hold reverence for rabbits. This is because Ostara is the Goddess of spring, and one of her forms was believed to be a rabbit.

Rabbits were seen as beacons of fertility because of their successful mating. Colored eggs were made as offerings to Ostara, because of their relation to fertility. This holiday is where the Christian holiday Easter originates.

The following are common Ostara traditions:

- Honoring the hare

Sacred to Goddess Ostara

Represents rebirth and spring

This eventually became the Easter Bunny

- The egg

Like all seeds, contains the potential of the Universe Symbolizes the balance between light and dark, female and male, Goddess and God

Bury egg by the front door to bring prosperity in the coming year

Color eggs with plant dyes and write rune/ sigil for fertility, health, love, etc., then you can hide them and have an Ostara egg hunt for the children

Beltane/ May Day – May 1Jst

This is the last of the spring fertility festivals and revels in the return of the full force of the Sun for summer. It is now that the sexuality of the Earth is at its highest because all life is exploding with robust fertility. Beltane also marks the time when the God falls in love with the Goddess and takes her as his bride, symbolizing the Sacred Marriage – the amalgamation of Earth and Sky.

Beltane is considered a fire festival, honoring not only passion and sexuality, but the birth of new ideas, dreams, and hopes – it honors life. There are a few common traditions done during Beltane:

- Handfasting (marriage)

Since this day symbolizes the Sacred Marriage, many others choose this day for their weddings as well

The ceremony is unique to couples, but always includes the tying of their hands together in a figure- eight with red ribbon or cord, and then toward the end of the ceremony it is unbound, symbolizing their choice to stay with the other.

Jumping the broom is also common. This comes from those in the past who were unable to pay for a church ceremony; they were accepted by their community as married if they literally jumped a broom that was placed on the ground.

Mead is typically the drink of choice, as it's the oldest drink known to man and considered the Brew of the Divine.

A-Maying

Couples spend the night with each other in the woods, making love and bringing back the first May/ hawthorn flowers to decorate their homes with

During any other time of year, hawthorn is considered unlucky

Young ladies made May Baskets and flower crowns as gifts

Daisy chains are the easiest for flower crowns

Maypole

Often made from birchwood, this pole was placed in the Earth to represent the potency of the God, and the ring of flowers around the top represents the Goddess and her fertility. The ribbons that adorn the Maypole, along with the weaving dance represent the union of the God and Goddess – Sky and Earth – and the circular nature of life.

Midsummer/ Litha – June 2Jst

Litha is also known as the summer solstice.

This holiday is a celebration of the God, represented by the Sun, so this holiday occurs on the longest day of the year – the summer solstice. It's at this time the Earth abounds with fertility, but it is also acknowledged that the Sun's power is beginning to fade. Wiccans who believe in the duality of the God, believe it is at this time the Oak King, the abundantly rich, will surrender to the Holly King and allow him to reign for the coming months. Those who believe in the Triple God view this as the beginning of the decline for the God as he prepares to enter the third stage of his life. Of course, this isn't meant to be a sad holiday, because all aspects of life are beautiful and have their purpose – so they celebrate. It's considered the perfect time of year for rituals centering around divination, protecting the family and home, and honoring the prime of the Oak King's life.

Litha, unlike most other Sabbats, isn't considered a harvest or fertility festival; it's simply time for honoring and celebrating. Regardless of the particular strand of Wicca being followed, the following traditions are common:

The Bonfire

On the eve of Midsummer, it was traditional to stay up all night to watch the Sunrise.

On hills and at sacred places, bonfires were lit to honor the Sun and its strength and fullness.

Herbs scattered into the fire to create aromatic atmosphere while people danced and jumped through the fire

Worship of the Oak

Worshipping trees has always played a big role in Litha, and they are usually decorated.

Oak trees are representative of the God or Oak King

Lammas– August 1st

Depending on the tradition, this holiday is also known as Lughnasadh and Lugnasad occurring between the 1st and 2nd of August.

This holiday symbolizes the first of the three harvest festivals of the year and brings attention to the harvesting of gardens and crops as people prepare for the upcoming winter. This is the period when the days begin to shorten, signifying the Sun Gods loss of strength as he begins to relinquish his control for the winter. It's also representative of the union between Sun and Earth as the Goddess has provided the First Harvest.

Since people are beginning to harvest their crops, this Sabbat usually includes a great celebratory feast. It is a time to honor Lugh, the Celtic God of Light, and give thanks for all the abundance of the year. It's known that although the cold months are approaching, there are already seeds in the Earth preparing to bloom again in the new year. Everything is cyclical and comes in its own time.

Regardless of tradition, the following practices are common on Lammas:

Cutting of the Grain

Cutting both the first and last grain are equally significant

The first would typically be cut at dawn and baked into Harvest Bread to be had at the feast and was considered as the God relinquishing his life so the community could continue on The last was usually turned into a corn dolly, kept in one's home near/ above the hearth until the next year's harvest

Mabon – Autumnal Equinox (September 2Jst)

This holiday is the perfect counterpart to Ostara and celebrates the God reaching his third phase of life as the Wise Man. Though this holiday is melancholier than most, it's a time for giving thanks for all the abundance received throughout the year. Wiccans tend to use this time to do work for their communities, giving back.

Mabon is the second of the three harvest festivals and is seen as a time for well-deserved rest after working hard for their harvest.

For those who believe in the Triple God, when the last of the grain has been cut, the God dies, joining the Crone in the Underworld to await his rebirth at Yule. Though somber, it is the knowledge he will return again that warrants celebration instead of sadness. Those who believe in the duality of the God see this as the time when the Holly King kills the Oak King and returns to power for the next 6 months, signaling the beginning of longer nights and shorter days.

Wiccans also use this time for reflection, looking back on the planning they'd done at the beginning of the year and seeing how those goals manifested over the year. It's a time for clearing out the old, completing projects, and sowing the seeds of new hopes and ideas – and though they lie passive for the winter, they are growing in the dark, waiting for the return of spring.

A few common traditions of Mabon are:

The Great Feast

A time for celebration with family and friends, relying primarily on vegetables and fruit locally grown

Clearing out

Prepare your home for the upcoming winter by removing unnecessary clutter,

so you have a peaceful environment for the contemplative period to come

Walk in Nature

Esbats

These are the other Holy Days, occurring monthly and typically corresponding with the Full Moon, though it's not a necessity. The important part is that rituals are performed at night as they're under the Moon with the power of the Goddess.

Esbats are the time to commune and connect with Deity, using the phases of the Moon to infuse magical workings pertaining to the upcoming month.

Waxing Moon

During the waxing Moon, rituals concerning pulling things to you are performed. This is the time to increase positive influence, work magic pertaining to increasing love, luck, abundance, and prosperity.

Waning Moon

During the waning Moon, rites pertaining to diminishing or dispelling things from one's life are performed.

This is a time to decrease negative influences and even removing people from one's life.

Full Moon

The full Moon represents the pinnacle of magical workings, enabling a Witch to perform practically any ritual s/he wants.

The full power of the Goddess is represented in the full Moon, allowing powerful magic to be worked.

New Moon

Also called the Dark Moon, this is a time for performing rituals involving intense protection. Those that practice dark or black magic also use the new Moon to power their magic, though one should always be wary of entertaining the thought of dark magic, as the Threefold Law applies to everyone.

Performing am Esbat

A coven, circle, or solitary practitioner gathers at a ritual space, casting a Sacred Circle that allows the Witches to both raise their psychic and magical power.

It is typically begun by speaking the Charge of the Goddess and the Wiccan Rede while inside the circle, beginning the nights ritual.

Whether in a group or alone, there is time spent using divination magic (Tarot, scrying, runes, etc.), rejoicing with drink and food as plans are made for the month ahead, and meditation alongside the ritual's purpose.

At the rituals close, libations are offered to Nature as thanks, either laid upon the Earth or buried, the circle is closed, and the ritual is officially over.

Chapter 2 The History of Witchcraft in Wicca

Ancient Inspirations

Witchcraft in the Wiccan tradition started with Gerald Gardner, who actually referred to his tradition as the Craft (short for Witchcraft). He and those who helped him develop and advocate for Wicca were partly inspired by ideas, practices, beliefs, and knowledge from ancient civilizations.

It was with the discovery of cave paintings, estimated to be 30,000 years old that shows a pregnant woman in the middle of a circle formed by eleven others and a man with a stag's head, that it was feasible to interpret this painting as the Goddess and God. Many believe Witchcraft is arguably the oldest practice, predating Christianity by 28,000 years. Many even refer to Witchcraft as the Old Religion, believing its traditions have been handed down over hundreds of years, going into hiding as the persecution of Pagans by the Christian Church were at their height.

Those who practiced Witchcraft in ancient history were knowledgeable about medicines and herbs, were in-tune with Nature and were seen as Shamanic healers in their communities. They were very aware humans weren't above Nature (the Earth and its creatures), but instead are parallel to them, one piece in a giant puzzle.

Gardner and his colleagues also used information from the occult revival in the UK during the 13th and 1Qth centuries to inspire Wiccan tradition, though much of the religion is based on reconstructions of the Irish, Welsh, and Scottish pre-Christian traditions. This was because a substantial amount of information was lost when the medieval church worked to eradicate its history.

The term 'Witch' has had negative connotations for hundreds of years, constantly being associated with heathenism, evil, and unrighteousness, much of this inspired by the Christian church's persecution of practitioners of the Craft.

Modern Inspirations

Modern Wiccan Witchcraft still has many of its ancient roots, but over the decades since its inception in the ¢0s and 50s, many practitioners have begun building their own form of the Craft, working with pantheons, Deities, magic, and tools that work for them, along with focusing heavier on Nature.

Gardner added aspects to Gardnerian Wicca that he related to or enjoyed (i.e. nudity and duality of the Goddess and God).

Modern Witches realize that Wicca isn't the be-all-end-all in achieving spirituality and that we are all allowed to follow the path that suits us best – keeping in mind the Five Points of Wiccan Belief.

The Five Points of Wiccan Belief

The Wiccan Aide

This is generally the go-to for the basic rules governing the religion

Its most common form is 'An it harm none, do as ye will'. This means that as long as the magic being done doesn't hurt yourself or any other living being (physically, emotionally, or mentally), you may practice as you wish

The Rede also contains information regarding Sabbats and other Wiccan practice

Most things in the Rede are regarded as common sense

The Three-fold Law/ Law of Aeturm

This is also encompassed in the Rede

'Ever mind the rule of three, what you put out comes back to thee'

This means whatever magic you put out into the Universe will come back to you three times stronger than the spell you cast

The Ethic of self-Responsibility

Simply put, this means accepting responsibility for one's mistakes

No one else to push the blame onto, i.e. devils, Gods, etc.

Plays into the Law of Return

Whatever energy we put out into the world will come back to us, so it's solely our responsibility to maintain positivity

The Ethic of Constant Improvement

This encompasses not only self-improvement but improving the Earth as well

Ecology is an important facet of Wicca because Nature is considered Divine

This doesn't just include helping the Earth's physical properties

Preaching, teaching, and actively living racial harmony and tolerance

Maintaining veneration for history and art Living peacefully

The Ethic of Attunement

Attunement is typically the goal in most rituals Being in-tune with Divinity

Three things Wiccans believe to be Divine Gods and Goddesses

Seen as more parental figures than jealous or vengeful gods

There to guide

Self

No one has the power to control the Self, except the 'owner' of the body

Universe

This includes the Earth, animals, plants, microbes, harvest cycles – all laws of the Universe are Divine

Even with the increase in Wicca's popularity, it's difficult to accurately determine how many practicing Wiccans there are. The number ranges from 300,000 to 3 million. A lot of this has to do with underrepresentation in poll and census forms, particularly a few decades ago, as Wicca wasn't recognized as a religion by the law until 1986 in the Dettmer v. Landon court case.

Magical Tools

Magical tools are anything used during rituals and spellwork, and though the list is long and varied, there are a few basic items most Wiccans use regularly.

It's important to consecrate all ritual tools before use, cleansing any stuck energies, and preparing them for your own use. Some Witches also find it important to claim possession over their tools, connecting them to themselves magically.

All of these items can be found online, in specialty Wiccan shops, New Age shops, and some even in your local grocery store.

Altar

Altars are typically the focal point of ritual acts, particularly with solitary practitioners. They're also used during Sabbats to honor specific aspects of Deities and give thanks. These can simply be seasonal or be up year-round.

An altar is simply a table that can be used for magical workings and can hold ritual tools.

Athame

An athame is typically a double-edged, dull knife with a dark or black handle that is used during rituals to direct energy – never for actually cutting anything. The athame can be engraved with runes or sigils to heighten power but isn't a necessity.

Athames are usually used to represent the God and are linked to Fire because of their phallic nature.

Besom

A besom is simply a broom made of birch twigs, willow binding, and a staff made of ash, though any natural materials can be used to create a Witch's broom.

The besom is linked to Water because both are considered purifiers. For this reason, they are used to both clean physical dirt and negative energy from a ritual space. This is important so that any leftover energy accrued during the last ritual or the time between cleaning can be removed, so it doesn't affect the success of future magical work.

Bell

Bells are used to bring unity to a magical circle because sound (vibration) can be a massive power source. The vibrations can ward off evil spirits, an idea that's been believed for hundreds of years. Some Witches also choose to use bells to invoke the Goddess and start and end a ritual.

Boline

A boline is another knife, though this one is used for physically cutting things, not directing energy, though it can still be used inside the circle if need be. A boline can be used to cut cords, wands, and herbs, along with inscribing sigils and runes into objects. It's typically a knife with a white handle as opposed to the athame with a dark handle.

Book of shadows

This can also be called a Grimoire and is a workbook containing notes, runes, spells, invocations, etc. that have worked (or not) for a Witch. It is used as a journal of sorts to keep track of a Witch's work and is extremely personal.

Cauldron

Traditionally cauldrons were used for brewing potions and cooking and are connected to Water and the Goddess.

This correlation occurs because the cauldron represents fertility, transformation, and femininity – all things the Goddess and Water also represent.

They are typically (and traditionally) made of cast iron with three legs.

Cauldrons serve multiple purposes, making it a focal point of ritual.

Censer/ Incense Burner

A censer is simply an incense burner used for ceremony and ritual that can typically be carried around the circle, though any cup or bowl can substitute as a censer. On altars, they are generally put in front of Deity images. Censers and incense burners are linked to Air.

Incense can be used to alter the state of consciousness to be more in line with the ritual work to be done, so choosing incense that corresponds to the magical work to be done is always useful.

Chalice

A chalice and a cauldron can serve similar goals; a chalice is simply smaller. It, like cauldrons, is connected to Water and is a symbol of fertility and the Goddess.

Some Witches choose to use chalices to contain saltwater cleanse used to consecrate objects, mix potions, and hold liquid related to the ritual (i.e. wine).

Deities

Out of respect, we would never actually classify these as 'tools,' but they are used to remind us of the Divine.

Many choose to place images of Goddesses and Gods special to them, or even objects that represent them, on their altar. Many believe adding these allow the Divine to live there, creating a living temple out of your altar. This is because statues of Goddesses and Gods have been said to hold Divine vibrations.

Directional Candles

Most Wiccans choose to have a candle for each of the Sacred Elements, often following a simple color-coding, as these can be used to hold and invoke the powers of each Direction.

North – Earth: green, black, or brown   East – Air: yellow

South – Fire: red or orange   West – Water: blue or aqua

Centre – Spirit: silver, white, or gold (where you aren't using Goddess/ God candles)

Goddess and God Candles

Unlike the directional candles, these are used to represent and invoke the powers of the Divine. These are usually pillar candles, which are taller than the others, and are placed on opposite sides of the pentacle or near the altar's center.

The God can be represented by a gold pillar candle, while the Goddess can be represented by white or silver. If one wishes to represent the Triple Goddess, use the following:

Maiden – white   Mother – red   Crone – black

Mortar and Pestle

A mortar and pestle are very practical tools used to grind herbs for spell work, potions, and creating one's own incense. They can be

made of wood, stone, ceramic, etc. and are fairly common to all traditions.

Most recommend using separate mortars for mundane vs. magical work since some herbs used in spell work can be toxic/ poisonous if ingested.

Paten

Also called a libation dish, this is used to give offerings of cake and wine to the Goddess and God and can be a flat plate or a cup/ bowl. If done in ritual and not just for your altar, bury the libations in the Earth at the close of the ritual. This ensures your offerings reach the Divine.

Pendulum

A pendulum is used for meditation and divination, where questions are formed in ways that answers come in counterclockwise and clockwise movements. Pendulums are fairly heavy objects (metal, stone, etc.) connected to a chain or strap, enabling them to swing back and forth.

Some Witches choose to use smaller pendulums for radiesthesia and dowsing as well.

Pentacle

A pentacle is a plate or disk inscribed with a sigil/ rune/ symbol (mostly a pentagram).

Pentagrams have existed in magic for millennia and are five-pointed stars that represent the Five Sacred Elements – Earth, Air, Fire, Water, and Spirit. It's typically used for invocation and protection, and some believe it to be a doorway between the Spirit World and our own.

Aobe

Robes are used in ritual to separate oneself from everyday life and enter the ritual mindset. Ritual robes can be adorned in sigils or symbols important to the Witch, or if the robe is from a coven, they typically add belts or special bits as one moves further in their studies. It isn't uncommon to wear nothing under the robe, as many see clothing as restrictive during magical workings.

Salt Water

This can be held in a chalice or just a small bowl or cup and will be used for cleansing the ritual space and any objects necessary for the spell work to be done.

Saltwater is unique because it represents both Water and Earth energies. It is generally placed in the center of an altar, as it represents the womb of the ocean, which birthed all life on Earth.

Scrying Mirror

This is a divination tool used for scrying, as well as consecrating objects with its reflective surface until one can see visions in the glass. A dark bowl, mirror, or ball is typically used for this practice.

Stones/ Crystals

Most Wiccans use crystals and stones in their practice, because they bring Earth's energy for grounding, along with qualities specific to each stone/ crystal. These will be discussed more in-depth in the following chapters.

Wand

Wands have been used as magical tools to direct energy for millennia. They can create sigils or magical symbols, cast Sacred Circles, etc. and are linked to Air.

Traditionally they were made from elder, willow, or oak, but any natural wood can be used. Some Witches even choose to add crystals onto the tip of the wand to amplify the energy being sent through the wand.

Chapter 3 Wiccan Traditions and Practices

Popular Wiccan Traditions

There are many different offshoots of Wicca, but there are 6 that are the most well-known, if not the most common anymore.

Gardnerian

Gerald Gardner is generally referred to by many as the 'father of Wicca' (1Q5¢), though he never actually named his religion Wicca (though he did occasionally call his members 'the Wicca' when he spoke of them collectively), and it wasn't until the religion made its way to North America that the name Wicca became common. He referred to their practices as Witchcraft when he started the Bricket Wood Coven, taking an amalgamation of experiences and sources he'd found or lived himself.

He spent time with the New Forest Glen Coven before he began his own, and used many of their ideas, rituals, and practices in what is now known as Gardnerian Wicca. He chose to have his coven consist of 13 members led by a High Priestess with her second in command being the High Priest.

He did this to symbolize the Goddess and God within the Sacred Circle, along with showing that the Goddess and God were counterparts to each other, as Gardner was the one to introduce the idea of a duo theistic religion.

He was also an avid nudist and incorporated that into his tradition. The more orthodox of Gardnerian covens still practice this aspect today.

In keeping with the rather stringent rules, Gardnerian Witches place a lot of importance in using the original Book of Shadows that Gardner wrote for magic and rituals; a few forms have been

published over the years even though it was supposed to be kept secret. Their rituals are also considerably more elaborate than other strands of Wicca, often involving ritual sex, though it's unknown if currently practicing Gardnerian still follow this tradition.

There are also three degrees of initiation, and anyone who would like to start their own coven within Gardnerian Wicca is required to have all three completed before. It's likely that Gardner took this practice for secret societies like the Hermetic Order of the Golden Dawn and the Freemasons. They were also among the most secretive covens, making it almost impossible for inquisitive outsiders or newcomers to learn anything about them.

To this day, traditional Gardnerian Wiccan covens are strictly initiatory; this means the only way one can join their coven is to be initiated by another Gardnerian. This allows them to continue being able to trace their lineage back to the original Bricket Wood Coven.

Alexandrian

This Wiccan tradition was started by Alex and Maxine Sanders in the UK in the 1Q60s. They were first initiated into the Gardnerian tradition in the 60s into one of the first Gardnerian covens. The name 'Alexandrian' was actually coined by Stewart Farrar, a fellow Witch, and friend for two reasons: a.) because of Sander's name, and b.) in adoration for the Library of Alexandria because of the amount of occult knowledge that was housed there.

There are a few similarities between Alexandrian and Gardnerian: Requires 3 degrees of coven initiation

Coven led by a High Priestess

Belief in supreme God and Goddess

Alexandrian tradition, though, brings about the worship of Deities –

i.e. the Holly and Oak Kings. There is also more emphasis placed on Hermeticism (an ancient mystic tradition) and ceremonial magic, along with facilitating many adjustments and changes. Alexandrian Wicca wasn't as strict as its predecessor, and though it does put some emphasis on following and respecting tradition, there's more focused on being open to growth. Because of this, it's less dogmatic, allowing followers to practice their own path.

Dianic

Women who joined Wicca because they were drawn to the idea that Deity could be female and equal to the God inspired the shift toward feminism when they were met with the harsh reality of misogynism within the ranks of the tradition.

It was the US in the 70s that brought about the shift to a Nature- based, feminist movement from the traditional Pagan, magic-based practice it used to be.

They stressed the importance of environmentalism, which was a popular topic for the 'hippies' of the time as well.

Dianic Wicca was founded by Zsuzsanna Budapest in the US. This was the first tradition to put their sole focus on the Goddess, though now the only coven who only accepts female Witches is the original coven (Susan B. Anthony Coven) started by Budapest in 71.

Dianic covens put a strong significance on being cognizant of the injustices and oppression women faced both socially and politically, making it a very feministic coven. For this reason, there isn't usually

a hierarchy. Compared to other traditions, they are more relaxed regarding the movement in the coven and spiritual growth. They do take part in the Sabbats and Esbats, but the magical workings that happen reflect a feminine approach in everything.

Seax

This tradition was founded in the US by Raymond Buckland, a Witch originally from the UK, in the 70s. He founded the first Gardnerian coven in the 60s in New York after being a High Priest in the UK.

Although, upon starting the coven in the US, he realized the structure of having a hierarchy inspired battles over ego, leading him to found Seax Wicca as a way to practice Gardnerian tradition in a way that worked for American culture.

His inspiration for Seax Wicca came from the Witchcraft of the Anglo-Saxons from the 5th and 11th century. They tend to focus their worship on Woden and Freya, the Goddess and God from Gardnerian Wicca. Although Seax was inspired by Gardner's original tradition, there are many differences between the two:

No secrecy

Sabbats and Esbats are typically open to all interested

An oath of secrecy isn't needed

Focus on studying various forms of divination and herbal lore

Constant adding of new material

Leaders of the coven are voted in democratically and are only allowed to lead for 1 lunar year (13 full Moons)

Lineage is unimportant

No degrees for initiation

An acceptable and recognized entry point is self-dedication

Norse

Though this path is relatively new, the tradition is centuries old, stemming from practices, beliefs, and Deities from ancient Norse customs in Scandinavia.

There isn't one specific founder, though the Eddas (Nordic mythology and poetry) were written in the 1300S. Those who follow the Norse tradition are typically inspired by the old sagas (i.e. Grimnismal) and feel connected to the Deities associated with the Nordic peoples. It's also common for Norse Wiccans to adopt Germanic and Nordic versions of the Sabbats.

Druidic and Celtic

These two forms of Wicca technically are two separate traditions, but over time people have begun incorporating aspects of both into their practice.

There isn't much known about the religious and magical traditions of the Druids, as the majority of their knowledge was passed on orally. We do know they were a staple of Celtic life, in the class of priests – philosophers, poets, and healers – who worked magic and divination. They believe everything is connected and all of Nature is intrinsically Divine. It's likely Druids inspired the surviving practices that are now incorporated into Celtic Wicca.

Celtic Witches honor a pantheon of Celtic Deities from Cornish, Gaulish, Welsh, and Irish, along with using the Sabbats Celtic names.

Both traditions are more shamanistic that more orthodox strands of Wicca and they put particular pertinency behind rune work, sacred stones, and herbal magic. Both are also more likely to have an egalitarian structure as opposed to a hierarchy.

Forms of Practice

Wicca differs from other religions because you can't simply find a mosque, church, or temple to seek out those who could answer your questions. Wicca is a fairly secretive practice, so you're unlikely to find advertisements for them in your local paper or bulletin. What you can do is a bit dependent on where you live. There could potentially be practicing covens or circles that could provide you with information based on the member's personal experiences.

In the age of the Internet, starting there can be the easiest way to find your answers. Add to that community listing in local newspapers and local New Age or specialty shops, and you may end up finding a group of Wiccans in your area. If not, there are many online communities of Wiccans, and though you may not be able to form a traditional circle or coven, you will have access to a network of people on a similar path to your own.

Covens

The word originally comes from the Latin word meaning "come together," and in the Middle Ages was used to describe any kind of gathering.

It wasn't until the 1600S that the word became associated with Witches.

The traditional idea of a coven involved 13 members, including a High Priestess and High Priest, to represent the Goddess and God, who would meet to secretly work magic and worship their Deities. There are many traditional covens around today that can still trace their lineage back to the original covens started by Alex Sanders and Gerald Gardner.

Covens are a fairly structured form of practice, requiring a serious time commitment because they meet to observe the Sabbats and Esbats along with other High Holy days or celebrations. There are also informal gatherings between these meetings that may or may not require attendance – though more often than not they will.

This is because every member is crucial to the rest of the coven. With the addition or subtraction of a person, the magical energy of the circle changes, which can affect the magical workings.

There are many covens who don't have specific ties to any one tradition, choosing instead to pull from many different traditions. They tend to adopt a less hierarchical leadership structure in favor of more egalitarian methods. This, put simply, meant instead of having one or two coven members who ran everything based potentially on their own lineage, they instead choose to be fairly democratic, electing the heads of their covens through impartiality.

Regardless of the coven's tradition, most hold a formal initiation ritual for their new members. This typically happens after practicing and studying for a year and one day, ensuring to the other coven members that you: a.) are dedicated to the Craft and the coven after having sufficient time to think it over, and b.) are able to participate in group rituals with a strong base of knowledge.

Most covens also follow degree systems for moving on to further study, allowing them to acquire a second and third degree within the coven. Upon the first initiation, one receives their first degree, and from there further study can be pursued – which is always encouraged.

Benefits

- Powerful magic is achievable
- Connecting spiritually and raising power becomes easier Communal energy
- Self-expression can be practiced safely in a closed-group environment
- Deep bonds form between members as their souls are opened during rituals together

Limitations

- Dogmatism
- Stagnancy as set patterns and accepted belief s are reinforced
- Battles caused by ego
- Self-aggrandizement
- Personality cults

Circles

Circles aren't as formal as covens; allowing members to come and go as they wish (for the most part). These groups are useful for someone who would like to meet other like-minded people, but isn't quite ready to make the leap to join a coven. There are often many varying levels of experience throughout a circle, so gaining knowledge and contributing your own ideas and perspectives can be easier.

Circles often meet to learn more about the Craft and are typically less concerned with always gathering to celebrate the Sabbats and Esbats

– and even less so with regular attendance. There are many circles which allow members to drop in and out as they please, or even just a tightknit group of friends.

Benefits

- New group members bring enthusiasm and fresh ideas Keeps members grounded by questioning patterns and ideas that have been established and practiced for a while
- Typically practice inclusivity

Healing to both members and Earth's soul

Recognition that we are all equal

Limitations

- Changing membership can make it hard to develop trust and a sense of community to do deeper spiritual work
- Everyone brings separate energy to the group, and when that changes that group's energy has to change as well, which can make members feel their magic isn't getting anywhere

Solitary Practitioners

This practice has surged more recently, and a majority of Wiccans practicing in the 21st century consider themselves solitary practitioners. This simply means they practice only with the company of the Divine.

Some choose to practice this way because they aren't able to find any person or groups in their area that follow the Wiccan path. Others choose this route because they enjoy learning the wonders of the Universe and the Divine alone and find it more rewarding that way.

That's not to say solitary Witches never interact with others of the same faith. Just because they choose to do the majority of their practice alone, they often gather with other solitaries to celebrate the Sabbats and Esbats, and that doesn't mean they lose their solitary practitioner status. It's also not uncommon for a solitary Witch to eventually become initiated, whether it be with a circle or coven, or by performing their own initiation ritual. Some even believe the Goddess can initiate solitary practitioners spontaneously.

Benefits

- Only serving your Deities
- Able to practice in a way that you connect with
- Able to commune with the Divine without taking on the energy of others

For extremely sensitive Witches, solitary practice is the only way for them, because group work can overwhelm them

- Able to perform unorthodox and spontaneous rituals

Limitations

- It can be difficult to stick to practice on one's own
- Solitary practitioners aren't able to raise as much energy as a coven or circle
- Having no guides/ mentors can stunt spiritual growth at a certain point

Eclectic Wicca

Eclectic Wicca or an eclectic Witch is an extremely broad term, encompassing any Witchcraft tradition that doesn't belong to a specific category.

This means they typically pull from multiple different traditions to create something that resonates with them.

There are those Witches who believe only practitioners who have a lineage that can be traced back to the original covens can be considered Wiccan, and those who are considered eclectic are actually Neowiccan – meaning those who practice a newer form of Wicca/non-traditional.

There are many solitary practitioners who choose an eclectic path and even a few covens as well. They can have quite varied reasons for choosing the term eclectic to describe their path, but a few are most common.

Modified Traditions

This could be any person, coven, or circle based off an established tradition, but has modified it significantly in their form of practice.

Mixed Traditions

Covens, circles, or solitary practitioners may pull from a variety of traditions and pantheons to make a 'blended' practice.

Individual Practices

A solitary practitioner may create their own tradition through various practices and beliefs, making it unable to be defined as a particular, already established form of the Craft.

It's also possible Witches yet to be initiated using publicly available material that isn't considered initiatory material, making the practice recognized as eclectic.

Potential Problems

Eclectic Witches mix various different traditions, beliefs, and pantheons, and while this can produce a richer experience, it can also cause problems. If an eclectic Witch doesn't ensure all of the practices s/he is combining harmonize together, all s/he is doing is diluting the magic of every tradition they work with.

This makes it imperative that a lot of thought and research goes into each practice one would like to add to their tradition because without a solid understanding supporting the beliefs behind the different systems, the magical workings you attempt may be weakened or not work at all.

Eclectic Wicca vs. Eclectic Witchcraft

There is a difference between the two, though the principle is still the same; Eclectic Witchcraft combines various elements from established traditions, just as Eclectic Wicca. An Eclectic Wiccan can practice a mix of Gardnerian and Alexandrian Wicca, or even a blend of Wiccan tradition and an entirely different magical path.

Regardless of the form of Wicca, as long as they believe in Deity, they are generally accepted as Wiccans.

Chapter 4 Candle Magic

What is Candle Magic

Candle magic is generally considered the best for beginning Wiccans and Witches attempting to flex their magical muscles. This is because seeing the flame burning can often aid beginning practitioners in visualizing the process of manifestation.

In candle magic you're using the flame as the medium to send your request – your intention/ spellwork/ thought – and as the candle burns your intention leaves the material or physical plane and enters the ethereal plane with your intention, allowing it to then manifest in the material plane, thus completing your magical will.

Candle magic works particularly well for beginners because they're a well-proportioned representation of the Elements. This allows for an easier connection to the Divine, making it more likely that beginning spellwork will garner results.

Elemental Representation

- Earth

The base and wick – needed to keep flame lit and grounded

- Water

The wax – changes from a solid to a liquid and then to gas, showing the changing characteristics of water

- Air

Oxygen needed to keep the flame burning and made visible by the smoke

- Fire

The flame – this is literal

- Spirit

By charging a candle with your will or intention will allow it to hold the collectivity of the Universe

The Magic of Color

Colors have their own magical associations, whether they be to qualities that are intangible or events like death, love, or luck. Using colors can strengthen and reinforce your magic, making your intention clearer.

Red

The color red is typically used for spellwork involving physical energy, love, willpower, and health because it's associated with strength, passion, intense emotions, and courage. This color is usually used to represent Fire in ritual.

Orange

The color orange is used in magic involving sudden changes and the ability to adapt to them, power, and encouragement. These work well with orange because of its association with vitality, energy, stimulation, and attraction. This color can be used in ritual to represent Fire.

Yellow

The color yellow is used in magic revolving around confidence, study, communication, and divination, because of its association with imagination, knowledge, inspiration, and intellect.

This color is usually used to represent Air in ritual.

Green

The color green is used in spellwork involving employment, health, fertility, good luck, and prosperity. This works well because of its association with growth, balance, abundance, renewal, and wealth. This color is usually used to represent Earth in ritual.

Blue

The color blue is typically used in magic to do with psychic ability, understanding, harmony at home, and healing due to its association to protection, truth, patience, peace, and wisdom. This color is usually used to represent Water in ritual.

Violet

The color violet is used in spellwork involving the balancing of sensitivity, divination, and increasing nurturing qualities. This is because of its association with wisdom, idealism, spirituality, devotion, and peace.

White

The color white is usually used in magical workings involving clarity, understanding, spiritual growth, cleansing, and the establishment of order due to its close association with innocence, peace, purity, and illumination.

Black

The color black is generally used in spellwork involving enlightenment, transformation, and the releasing and banishing of negative energies. This is made possible by black's association with stability, force, protection, and dignity.

Silver

The color silver is used in magic involving psychic and spiritual development, warding off negativity, and meditation due to its association with psychic ability, memory, intelligence, and wisdom. This color is often used to represent the Goddess in rituals.

Gold

The color gold is typically used in spellwork involving health, finances, divination, good fortune, success, and ambition due to its association with self-realization, intuition, inner strength, and understanding.

This color is usually used to represent the God in ritual.

Brown

The color brown is usually used in magic involving concentration, animal companions, balance, material gain, and home. This is because of its association with solidity, strength, grounding, and endurance. This color can be used to represent Earth in ritual.

Grey

The color grey is used in spellwork revolving around binding negative influence, making complex decisions, and reaching a compromise due to its association with contemplation, reserve, neutrality, and stability.

Indigo

The color indigo is generally used in magic involving spiritual healing, meditation, self-mastery, and having a clear purpose. This is because of its association with fluidity, emotion, expressiveness, and insight.

Pink

The color pink is typically used in spell work to do with partnerships, romance, spiritual awakenings, and children's magic due to its association with friendship, affection, spiritual healing, and companionship.

Copper

Copper is generally used in spellwork involving business fertility, monetary goals, and professional growth due to its connection to career maneuvers and passion.

Color and Astrology

You can use the corresponding color to an absent coven members astrology sign to represent them in the circle, or when casting a spell for someone else, that person can be represented with their corresponding candle color as well.

Mauve – Pisces

Any color – Aquarius

Black – Capricorn

Purple – Sagittarius

Red – Scorpio

Pink – Libra

Yellow – Virgo

Orange – Leo

Silver – Cancer

Yellow – Gemin

Green – Taurus

Red – Aires

Enhancing Candle Magic

Aside from using color correspondences to strengthen your spell work, there are a few other things you can do to increase the likelihood of success, most of which will be discussed in further depth in the coming chapters:

- Consecrating the candle with magically charged oil
- Rolling the oil-covered candle in herbs corresponding to your intention
- Inscribing the body of the candle with a sigil(s) that goes with your goal

Divine Communication Through Candles

Divine communication using candles is much like a form of divination. Witches may choose to watch the movement, shape, and flame size to gather signs of the potential of success for the spell.

Depending on the tradition one may believe:

- If the flame is strong and tall, the manifestation process is happening quickly
- If the flame is weak and low, there isn't a lot of spiritual energy being invested into the spell
- If the wick generates black, thick smoke, there is active resistance to the magical working – whether that be yourself, an outside force, unknown circumstances, or another person

Another form, aside from watching the candle while it's burning, is looking at the wax once it's melted. This form of magic is called ceromancy, so much like looking into a crystal ball, reading tea leaves, or using a scrying glass, you can interpret shapes in the melted wax of a candle you used for ritual/ spell work.

Just be careful not to overthink your interpretations, because the last thing you want to do is alter the direction or intent of the spell.

Spells and Rituals Using Candles

After you've decided the purpose of your spell, you'll need to choose a candle color that works with your intent. Using the lists above, you should be able to determine the right color for you.

Preparing for Your Candle Spell

1. Choose your candle color

a. Make sure it's unused

2. Charge candle with your intent

a. You can charge it with your own energy by holding the candle and visualizing your will as already accomplished

b. You can also consecrate the candle in essential oils that aid in the purpose of your ritual

i. The fragrances should be natural

ii. Starting at either the top or bottom of the candle, spread the oils in one direction while thinking of your intent

3. If you are using crystals to amplify your spell work, set these up now

Sample Candle Magic Spells

Confidence

You will need pure water (that you feel comfortable drinking), white and pink rose petals and a pink candle.

Using a table or your altar, create a circle of rose petals and put the candle in the center.

Focus on your best traits and think about those for a few minutes before lighting the candle.

Light the candle and repeat three times:

May I find my worth With Divine purpose

Take a decent drink of the water, imagining it carrying away all negative thoughts you have of yourself.

Let the candle burn down and bury the remnants in the Earth.

House/ Aoom/ Home Cleansing

You will need salt, a blue candle, and a piece of white paper cut into the shape of a square.

Using a table or your altar, place the paper onto it and put the candle in the center. Sprinkle the salt around the paper in a circle, so all ¢ corners are touching the salt.

Light the candle at the start of the hour (exactly 3:00, 4:00, etc.) and let it burn itself out. When done, sweep the salt on the paper and pour that down the drain, visualizing all the negativity leaving with it. Bury the paper in the Earth.

Drawing money 1

This spell will be done with the power of the full Moon, so the light should be able to shine into the room you're doing the spell in.

You will need 1 coin that contains silver (old dimes are a good choice), 7 fresh basil leaves, a ceramic bowl or cauldron, and spring/ rainwater.

Put your coin into your bowl and add water until it's half-full. Put the bowl somewhere the Moonlight will hit it while you continue the ritual.

One at a time, drop the basil into the water as you say:

As surely as the moon illuminates the night Will prosperity in wealth be mine

Leave the bowl overnight and pour it out the next morning in your yard. Keep the coin in your pocket.

Drawing money 2

You will need a coin (the higher denomination, the better), a green candle, bowline or another sharp tool, candle holder, and cinnamon and vanilla oils.

Use your bowline or any other sharp tool and inscribe the word 'wealth' onto the side of the candle. Using the vanilla and cinnamon oil, consecrate the word.

Place your coin in your candle holder and put the candle on top of it. Light the candle and let it burn itself out. When out, take the wax covered candle and put it somewhere safe.

Drawing money 3

You will need pine and patchouli incense, acorns (or smooth stones), 1 green candle, 1 gold candle, and 1 piece of paper.

Carve the Fehu rune into the bottom of both candles, then put them in candle holders opposite each other.

Put the patchouli incense by the gold candle and pine by the green. Light all four.

Draw Fehu onto the paper and place the stones or acorns over top. Let the candles burn themselves out, and then let the stones or acorns remain on your altar (or table) until wealth comes your way.

Home and Hearth Blessing

You will need a bell, 3 purple or blue candles (can be tea lights as long as the penny fits underneath them), 3 pennies (copper), and 3 incense sticks in rosemary, sandalwood, and frankincense.

Using a table or your altar, place the 3 candles in a triangle with 1 penny under each.

Light the first candle and say:

Bring hope to this home

Light the sandalwood incense and ring the bell.

Light the second candle and say:

Bring peace to this home

Light the frankincense and right the bell.

Light the third candle and say:

Bring good fortune to this home

Light rosemary incense and ring the bell a final time.

Put the incense in the center of the candle triangle and let it burn for an hour or more. Snuff the candles out when done.

Banishing Negativity

You will need sandalwood oil, 1 black candle, a mortar and pestle (or something to crush your herbs with), dried mint, and white sage.

Anoint your candle with the sandalwood oil, then roll the candle in the crushed herbs so the oil lets it stick to the candle.

Place the candle on a table or your altar and light it. Repeat these words three times:

By the powers of the Divine, May negative energy be gone,

May bad attitudes be gone, May poor spirits be gone,

May peace and harmony live in this space

Let the candle burn itself out, and bury the remaining wax in the Earth.

Lucid Dreams

You will need a piece of silver or purple fabric cut into the shape of a square, 1 WHITE candle, amethyst crystal, and a black marker.

Draw an eye on your candle, the amethyst, and the fabric with your marker.

Put everything on a table or your altar, with the stone sitting on the fabric so the eyes are touching, and then light the candle.

Imagine an eye on your forehead opening, allowing you to see your dreams. Take the fabric and hold it to your forehead, with the eye in the center of your forehead.

Focus on the candle and repeat:

Awaken sight

Do this three times, then put the fabric back. Allow the candle to burn itself out, then sleep with the fabric under your pillow.

Good Health

You will need 1 WHITE candle, 1 cinnamon stick, and 1 glass of organic apple juice.

Stir the juice with the cinnamon stick ¢ times clockwise, then light the candle.

Take 3 sips of the juice and repeat the following 3 times:

Let the Divine bless my body and soul Wellness and health are my goal

Drink the remaining juice and snuff the candle out.

Chapter 5: Crystal Magic

What Is Crystal Magic

Crystal magic is a common Wiccan practice, though it doesn't just involve 'crystals,' but a plethora of solid minerals, all of which technically fall under the "Wiccan crystal" umbrella. Because of this, crystals and stones are typically interchangeable terms for Wiccans and Witches.

Solid minerals are simply any substance that's inorganic and formed naturally in the Earth

Because many Wiccans believe crystals to be alive, containing a specific composition and energy signature, it makes sense they could be used as conduits, because all matter, whether visible or not (thought/ intention), is fundamentally energy.

Since crystals are believed to give healing energy not only to people, but plants and animals as well, they have the same power as other elements of Nature – flowing water, wind, soil, etc., and because of this, they can conduct energy.

This means that, like through the flame of a candle, you can send your intention out through the crystal's energy field.

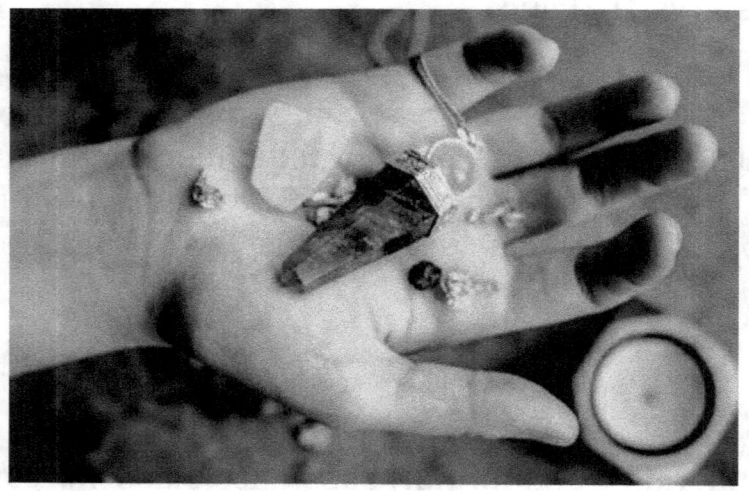

Crystals come in a multitude of colors, allowing the practitioner to naturally take advantage of color correspondences without having to use dyes – along with the crystal's own correspondences.

Popular Uses

- Divination
- Healing
- Protection
- Scrying
- Manifesting love, wealth, etc.

- Magical jewelry

- Honor Deities with their sacred stones
- Marking the Sacred Circle before beginning rituals
- In talismans, amulets, and other good luck charms

Acquiring Crystals

There are a few different places one can buy or find crystals, and it's all dependent on your preference. Many practitioners say the perfect crystal will choose you. This means that you will be drawn to the stone that's right for you. Whether you believe this or not, you have a few options for finding crystals near you:

- New Age/ Wiccan shops
- In Nature
- Shops focused specifically on stones and crystals
- Online retailers

Cleansing Your Crystals

This is an important step for many Wiccans, because it allows them to clear all energy, whether positive or negative, from the crystal before charging it with their own intention.

This gives the practitioner the ability to ensure their magical will isn't being altered by someone else's residual energy.

The only instance in which you wouldn't need to cleanse a new crystal would be if it was given to you already charged with a specific intent meant for you.

You should cleanse your crystals at least once a month, though if you're frequently using a crystal, it may need to be cleansed more than that. If you're adding a new intention or if it has been used for healing, it should be cleansed directly before and after its use.

Sunlight/ Moonlight Cleansing

Allow your crystals to bathe in the Sun or Moon for a minimum of ¢ hours once a month.

Crystalized Cleansing with Quartz or Selenite

Place your crystals on clear quartz for 6 or more hours. Optionally use a selenite charging plate for crystal jewelry. Place jewelry on the plate at night before bed so in the morning it will be ready to wear again.

Saging/ Smudging

Smudging involves the burning of frankincense or sage to cleanse crystals in its smoke. It is recommended that 20 to 30 seconds of smudging per crystal is sufficient.

Return to Nature

Earth has cleansing and grounding properties. By burying your crystals for 24 hours, you are allowing the soil to absorb all the built-up energy in the crystal. You can also use a source of running water for a few moments, so long as you keep the intention of cleansing in your mind.

Salt Water Cleanse

If you don't have access to sea water, you can simply mix water and sea salt in a glass bowl and place your crystals in this solution for 1 to 24 hours for a regular cleansing or up to a week for a deep cleanse. It's important to rinse your crystals with water to remove the remainder of the salt, and then dispose of the salt water, as it now contains all the negative energy pulled from the crystal.

Do not use salt water cleanse on:

- Porous crystals
- Crystals containing metal
- Crystals that already contain water
- Examples: opal, hematite, lapis lazuli, pyrite

Dry Salt Cleanse

Fill a glass bowl halfway with sea salt, then bury or simply place crystals on top. You can leave the crystals for hours, overnight, or days, all depending on the level of cleansing you need to be done. After the cleansing be sure to thoroughly rinse all crystals so there's no remaining salt, and dispose of the bowl of salt as it now contains all the remnants of negative energy pulled from the crystal(s). As with the salt cleanse, do not use on:

- Porous crystals
- Crystals containing metal
- Crystals that already contain water
- Examples: opal, hematite, lapis lazuli, pyrite

Non-Contact Salt Cleanse

This method of cleansing is the safest use of salt, meaning it can be used on crystals you couldn't otherwise cleanse with a salt method, along with crystals and stones in metal jewelry.

Fill a glass bowl 2/3 of the way with dry sea salt, then place a drinking glass or smaller glass bowl inside, so half of it is buried in the salt. You can then place the crystals into the smaller bowl/ glass and add distilled or mineral water so the crystals are just covered. This prevents the salt fumes from damaging the crystals. While this method does take longer since the salt isn't in direct contact with the crystals, it still works and is safe for all crystals.

Once you've allowed them to sit for your preferred amount of time, be sure to throw out the salt, as it has absorbed all the negative energies from the crystals.

Geode, Cluster, or Crystal Druse Cleanse

Clear quartz or amethyst crystals can be used to cleanse other crystals safely over the course of 24 to

48 hours. A clear quartz geode, cluster, or bed does provide a faster cleansing than amethyst, but both are equally effective. Quartz and amethyst are able to absorb and neutralize stored energy, then release the good energy stored inside itself into the crystals that have just been cleansed. This means now your crystal is both cleansed and energized at the same time.

Visualization Cleanse

This cleanse is possibly the simplest to do, because you're just using thought energy. To do this cleanse, begin by holding your crystal. Imagine a bright white light surrounding the crystal, turning into a beam of light passing through the stone and removing all of the crystal's stored energy. Continue this visualization until you feel the crystal has been thoroughly cleansed.

Chargimg Your Crystals

Charging your crystals is important because this is the only way it will continue to deliver its natural energy and vibrations. Charging your crystals with your own intent also allows them to be used in specific spells or rituals. You should charge your crystals before and after each use, or at least once a month.

Water Charging

If you have a source of running water near you, you can place your crystals in an open mesh bag and let the water run over them. Water is naturally cleansing, while also having energizing/ charging properties.

If you are unable to use running water, tap water will do as well. Place your crystals in a glass bowl or drinking glass and let the tap water run over them for 10 to 20 minutes.

As with salt cleanses, water charging cannot be done on crystals that:

- Are porous
- Have a high metal content

Sunlight and Moonlight Charging

Just like you can use Sunlight and Moonlight to cleanse your crystals, you can also use it to charge them, because of the natural energies they transmit.

Many Wiccans choose to do this directly after cleansing them, allowing the crystals to be charged by both the Sun and the Moon over the period of a few days.

- The Sun provides a strong, masculine energy
- The Moon provides a gentle, feminine energy

When using the Sun to charge crystals, be aware that the Sunlight may change the properties of certain crystals, like amethyst, and that certain colored crystals may fade over a period of time. Because of this, many choose to charge them during sunrise or sunset since the Sun's rays aren't as strong.

Physical Contact Charging

Native American crystal charging involves using your body's own energy to energize the stones. They believed by handling, picking up, or rubbing the crystal between the palm of your hand, you could direct your own energy into the stone.

Sound Bath Charging

Vibrations and frequencies hold their own form of energy, making them great for charging crystals.

The sound (vibrations) break up stored and/or stuck energy, thereby bringing back its harmony. Helpful sounds to charge:

- OM mantra
- Beethoven's 5th Symphony
- Tibetan singing bowls

Specific Programming

If you need to use your crystals for a specific ritual or spell, it is important to charge the crystal with that intent. The better you become at actively directing your thought energy, the easier this will become. By focusing on the energy you want to program the crystal with, you can transmit that energy directly into the stone. It's important to be direct and explicit in the intent you're placing in it because overloading the crystal will lead to a higher chance of failure.

Popular Crystals and Their Uses

There are hundreds of crystals, so explaining all of them would be an entirely separate book, so here we'll touch on the most common crystals and what they're typically used for.

Amethyst

- Color: Violet
- Uses: Clearing a sacred space, enhancing psychic abilities, calming, strengthening magical workings, sharpening intuition and mental focus, and assisting with sleep

Bloodstone

- Color: Green with flecks of gold and red
- Uses: Fertility, prosperity, abundance, and promoting physical healing

Hematite:

- Color: Gray/ silver/ shiny black
- Uses: Courage, reliability, optimism, grounding, balance, protection, stability, strengthening confidence and willpower and helping solve problems

Carnelian

- Color: Yellow

- Uses: Renewal, having useful dreams, and aiding in self-confidence

Citrine

- Color: Orange/ red
- Uses: Inspiring courage and warding off negative energy

Lapis Lazuli

- Color: Dark blue/ blue
- Uses: Meditation, communication, divination, and helping with altered consciousness

Jade

- Color: Green with flecks of gold/ red
- Uses: Harmony, protection from negativity, prosperity, abundance, promoting emotional balance, and wisdom

Jet

- Color: Black

- Uses: Protection from negativity and supporting transitions by centering and grounding

Quartz

- Color: Clear/ white
- Uses: Clarity, promoting healing, and spiritual development

Malachite

- Color: Green with stripes of black and dark green
- Uses: Supporting emotional courage and spiritual growth and helpful for big changes

Moonstone

- Color: Pale blue/ white
- Uses: Increasing psychic receptivity, creativity, and supporting wisdom and intuition

Rose Quartz

- Color: Pink
- Uses: Fertility, calming, forgiveness, promoting emotional healing, friendship, harmony, and love

Celestite

- Color: Light blue/ baby blue
- Uses: Calming, stress relief, astral projection, psychic abilities, and uplifting

Selenite

- Color: Transparent (can be green, grey, brown, or orange)
- Uses: Purification, serenity, meditation, peace, purity of heart, positivity, and universal consciousness

Tiger's Eye

- Color: Tan/ brown/ gold with black bands
- Uses: Increased energy and protection

Meteorites

- Color: Charcoal/ dark grey
- Uses: Strengthening body, physically healing, balancing and protecting emotions, and connecting with the Universe's energy

Galaxite

- Color: Yellow/ red, brown/ red, black

- Uses: Contacting and expanding higher realm, inner peace, balancing and protecting the aura, and restoring calm

Lepidolite

- Color: Lilac/ pink
- Uses: Releasing and reorganizing old psychological and behavioral patterns to induce change gently, balancing moods, helping in transitions, calming negative emotions, aiding in reducing depression, and emotional healing.

Pink Calcite/ Reiki Stone

- Color: Pink
- Uses: Promoting self-empowerment, helping achieve goals, happiness, increasing healing powers, and giving emotional stability

Amber

- Color: Orange/ yellow/ translucent/ brown
- Uses: Drawing pain out from the physical body, the mind, and the spirit, stimulating the body's

mechanisms to heal, and absorbing stagnant and negative energy

Aventurine

- Color: Green
- Uses: Increasing perception, intelligence, and creativity, releasing energy blockages and negativity, and health benefits for sinuses, liver, lungs, and heart

Onyx

- Color: Black
- Uses: Preventing the drain of personal energy, aiding the development of physical and emotional strength and stamina, and absorbing negative energy

Blue Agate

- Color: Blue with white lines/ blue

- Uses: Soothing and nurturing, aiding in the peace of mind and emotional healing, and boosting the ability to communicate

Emerald

- Color: Green
- Uses: Promoting friendship, bringing loyalty, enhancing unconditional love, increasing unity, keeping partnerships in balance, and effectively healing emotions

Fire Agate

- Color: Translucent deep red/ brown with flecks of green, red, gold, and orange
- Uses: Aiding in spiritual awakening, grounding and inspiring, aiding in courage to follow a spiritual path, promoting passion in life and love, protection, aiding in inner composure, stability, and maturity, and encouraging a high standard in others and one's self

Fluorite

- Color: Basically entire color spectrum, most commonly blue, green, purple, and yellow
- Uses: Improving coordination and balance both mentally and physically, neutralizing stress and negative energy, helping in decision making, and encouraging positivity

Green Garnet

- Color: Green
- Uses: Aiding in liberation, restoration, and growth, strengthening the commitment to spiritual growth or a higher purpose, increasing development, renewal, and development

Larimar

- Color: Light blue/ blue/ green-blue
- Uses: Facilitating outer manifestation and inner wisdom, aiding in healing emotionally, physically, mentally, and spiritually

Mother of Pearl

- Color: Gray/ white/ yellow/ silver

- Uses: Quieting and relaxing emotions, increasing inner peace, facilitating intuition, visualization, and imagination, aiding in harmonizing with Nature and the forces of the Universe, aiding in purification and regeneration

Moss Agate

Color: Green with brown/ white flecks

Uses: Aiding in new beginnings, reducing weather sensitivity, attracting an abundance wealth, aiding in refreshing the soul, and improving self-esteem

Obsidian

- Color: Black
- Uses: Enhancing truth, shielding against negativity and blocking psychic and physical attacks, and drawing out mental tension and stress

Pyrite

- Color: Gold/ brassy yellow with black and green streak
- Uses: Promoting physical well-being, good luck, shielding from environmental pollutants and

negative energy, and enhancing willpower and strength of mind

Snowflake Obsidian

- Color: Black with white flakes resembling snowflakes
- Uses: Balancing the spirit, mind, and body, aids in recognizing and releasing Stressful mental patterns, empowering loneliness, and isolation to aid meditation.

Spells and Rituals Using Crystals

Crystals can be used in spell work and rituals for practically anything under the sun. Writing your own spells, while they have the ability to work easier because of your connection to the words, can sometimes be a daunting task. Below you will find a few common rituals to help guide you.

Motivation

Crystal(s) to use: red jasper, tiger's eye

Steps:

1. Sit in a comfortable position

2.   Take deep breaths, focusing on slow, even breathing

3.   Hold the cleansed crystals in your hands and close your eyes

4. Ask yourself what aspects of your life you need to be actionable in

5.   Repeat this question and focus on the grounding, encouraging the energy of the crystals

6.   Do this until you feel motivated to move forward

Good Health

Crystal(s) to use: Bloodstone, quartz crystal

Steps:

1.   Sit in a comfortable position

2.   Take deep breaths, focusing on slow, even breathing

3.   Hold the cleansed crystals in your hands and close your eyes

4. Focus solely on your intent, visualizing that energy being infused in the crystals

5.   Repeat your intention until you feel you have charged your crystals

6. Leave them somewhere you see them often or carry them with you

Increased Creativity

Crystal(s) to use: carnelian heart, moonstone

Steps:

Clarity

1. Sit in a comfortable position
2. Take deep breaths, focusing on slow, even breathing
3. Hold the cleansed crystals in your hands and close your eyes
4. Chant: I am a creative being Q times

Clarity

Crystal(s) to use: crystal quartz

Steps:

Love

1. Place crystal on a windowsill where the Moonlight can reach it, or outside
2. When the Moon is full, sit outside with the crystal in your hands
3. Focus your intent

a. Guidance toward the highest manifestation of self

b. Aid in unraveling a problem

4. Remember to thank the Divine for their guidance

Love

Crystal(s) to use: rose quartz

Steps:

1. Sit in a comfortable position

2. Breathe deeply, focusing on calm, even breaths

3. Hold the crystal in your hand and close your eyes

4. Visualize how you would feel if the love you desired were in your life

a. Love of another

b. Self-love

c. Universal love

5. Chant: I ask the Goddess and God to manifest (specific love) in my life. I trust that your Divine knowledge will

Wealth

bring one worthy of the love I have to give.

6.   Repeat this 3 times, then keep the crystal near your bed

Wealth

Crystal(s): pyrite

Steps:

1.   Hold the crystal in your hand and focus on your intent

2.   Chant over the crystal:

a.   I am prosperous in monetary endeavors

b.   May wealth and abundance be brought to me

3.   Pass the crystal over something that represents money to you – actual money, a business contract, a business card, an employer's logo

4. Do this 3 times clockwise, repeating the chant of your choosing once more

5. Put the crystal somewhere you see it often, carry it with you, or leave it in your workspace

Protection

Crystal(s) used: black tourmaline, onyx

Steps:

Take a deep breath and clear your mind

Take your crystals in your hands and focus on your intent for a few moments

Feel your will infusing the crystals

Place one by your front door and visualize a bubble of light coming out from the crystal, shielding your home

Make sure you're focusing on your intent, only allowing positive energies to enter your space

Place the other crystal in your room a sacred space, or carry it with you, visualizing the same bubble protecting you

Psychic Ability

Crystal(s) to use: azurite

Steps:

Decide what you want to accomplish with your crystal Opening your third eye

Assisting you in divination magic

Recharging your third eye if you're feeling drained Take your crystal in your hands and chant your intent

By the Divine powers of the Goddess, I have awakened my third eye

By the Divine powers of the Goddess, allow this crystal to assist me in my (specific divination) magic By the Divine powers of the Goddess, allow this crystal to recharge and cleanse my energies, enabling me to continue in my psychic pursuits

Repeat the chant Q times, or until you feel your will has been infused into the crystal

Use this crystal in your magical work, or meditate with it between your eyebrows

Crystals, like most magical tools, can be used in conjunction with other forms of magic, i.e. divination magic, candle magic, herbal magic, etc.

You can use your infused crystal to inscribe a goal or rune into a candle, amplifying your will with the crystal's power. You can choose to empower your spellwork with quartz crystals, as they amplify magic, or you can even use them as constant staples on your altar or in your home.

Chapter 6: Herbal Magic

What is Herbal Magic

Much like crystal magic, herbal magic has a fairly broad scope. An herb is any plant that is useful, whether it is used for clothing, cooking, magical work, medicine, spiritual work, or fragrance. This also includes deadly/ toxic/ harmful plants. A few examples of herbs:

- Grasses
- Flowers
- Vegetables
- Fruits
- Trees
- Shrubs
- Henbane (toxic)
- Belladonna (toxic)

If working with toxic plants make you weary, there are usually always alternatives.

Herbal magic involves any kind of magic that uses an herb or blend of herbs to aid in their magical workings.

Many witches agree with Aristotle, who believed plants have 'psyches,' and though this is usually used to describe the spirit or soul of a human, many believe plants have a sort of consciousness as well.

This belief is somewhat backed by scientists, who through studies have shown plants cooperate and communicate with one another through roots and fungi that live underground.

This is even done from one species to another, and they use this to determine predators who may be nearby or to exchange nutrients so they can continue to grow.

For Wiccans and Witches, though, this is simply seen as the inherent intelligence Mother Earth possesses.

Herbal magic is a particularly practical form of magic because a lot can be done with ingredients you likely already have at home. Many Wiccans and Witches choose to use herbs for magical workings including:

- Marking the Sacred Circle before Sabbat rituals
- Honor patron Deities
- Dream pillows

- Spell jars
- Sachets
- Poppets
- Charms
- Incense
- Magical teas
- Tinctures
- Potions
- Baked goods and other foods
- Bath soaps/ teas
- House cleaner

Magic is rife with symbolism, and in herbal magic, plants represent the embodiment of the Four Sacred Elements creating and sustaining life together:

- Everything begins as seeds in the Earth's soil
- Minerals that sustain the seeds life are found there

- The 'Fire' of the Sun allows carbon dioxide to convert into oxygen, directly affecting the quality of Air

Air, in the form of wind, creates and spreads more life

Wind stimulates leaves and stems along with scattering seeds

- Water is crucial for all plant life

Plants also play an important role in Earth's water regulation cycles by helping move it from the Earth to the atmosphere

Learning About Herbs

Herbal magic can certainly be overwhelming when first starting out, based simply on the sheer number of herbs that exist. Because of this, it's easiest for those starting out to pick one or two herbs at a time to get familiar with. Doing it this way will allow you to build your relationship with each plant and the energies that go along with it.

If you can start your own herb garden, even better! This is the easiest way to connect with the Earth's energy because you are literally in touch with the Sun, Earth, rain, wind, and all the insects and animals that play a role in keeping up the cycle of life and death. It's also useful because you can infuse your intention into the herbs from the moment they're 'born.'

If you can't or don't want to start your own garden, many of the common/ popular herbs can be found in the spice section of your grocery store.

Popular Herbs Basil

Bay leaf

- Uses: Protection, fostering loving vibrations, and warding away negativity in the home

- Uses: Purification, healing, good fortune, protection, strength, success, and money

Chamomile

- Uses: Bringing healing and love, and relieving situations that are stressful

Cinnamon

- Uses: Prosperity, raising spiritual vibrations, luck, love, and success

Dandelion

- Uses: Interacting with the spirit world, divination, and wishes

Elecampane

- Uses: Protection, luck, communicating with plant spirits, and dispelling negative vibrations

Hibiscus Lavender

- Uses: Dreams, lust, divination, and love

Lavender

- Uses: Peace, restful sleep, healing and happiness, passion, money, relieving grief, meditation, clairvoyance, longevity, and protection

Mugwort

- Uses: Protection, increasing fertility and lust, psychic powers

Nutmeg

- Uses: Prosperity and money, protection, and good luck

Rosemary

- Uses: Promoting healthy rest, lust, and love

Sage

- Uses: Wisdom, protection, dispelling negative energy, and longevity

Star Anise

- Uses: Connecting to Spirit, lucky, magical and psychic power

Thyme

- Uses: Attracting loyalty, psychic abilities, and affection

Valerian

- Uses: Protection, purifying sacred space, driving away negativity

Chapter 7: Divination Magic

Common forms of divination magic are:

- Tarot

- Runes

- Scrying/ crystal gazing

- Dowsing

As with any magical tool, it needs to be consecrated before use. This not only ensures it's ready to be used, but also that it's blessed (in this case) by the Goddess in her lunar aspect.

This is because She has power over psychic ability.

The Tarot

As mentioned in the first chapter, a Tarot deck is made up of two Arcana, the Major and Minor, with the Major Arcana being the most powerful. All of these together with a total of 78 cards.

The art of reading the Tarot is learned with perseverance and time, as it can take several years to become adept in it. There are a few helpful tips for if you're just starting:

- Choose a deck that appeals to you
- Familiarize yourself with the Major Arcana first 0-21 (Tarot cards are numbered)

- Practice with simple questions first
- Ask the Divine, Deity, or the Spirit of Divination to assist you
- Use whatever you feel a connection to

Major Arcama Card Meamimgs

Use these to guide your interpretations, not do the divining for you.

The Fool

- Changing direction
- Use talents that are hidden
- Unexpected/ unplanned situation
- Beginning new enterprise/ cycle
- Moving toward a future that's unknown
- Look at all options before making decision

The Magician

- Prepared to take action

- Great energy and power at your fingertips Master of self
- Time to act
- Sudden solution

The High Priestess
- Feminine balance Occult learning
- Secrets that block the path and must be understood Intuition

The Empress
- Encourages love, compassion, and beauty
- Financial security
- Emotional stability
- Motherly love
- Womanly love
- Happiness
- Good fortune
- Pregnancy

The Emperor
- Authority and patriarchal
- thought Leadership
- Great power
- Can also denote being up against a strong force

The Priest/ Hierophant
- Karma
- Encourages finding spiritual perspectives on the situation
- The messenger from the Divine
- Encourages following the rules

The Lovers
- Close relationships
- Attention needed to love life
- A decision that needs to be made
- The choice between two opposing forces
- Several people affected by a decision

The Chariot
- Indication for upcoming victory

- Determination and drive
- Self-control Success

Strength
- Spiritual strength
- Ability to overcome a difficult situation
- Courage

Wheel of Fortune
- Upward mobility
- A reminder that nothing holds permanence
- Constant revolving nature of Fortune
- Unpredictability

The Hermit
- Spiritual enlightenment
- Answers will be found by looking within
- Introspection
- Carefully planning the next step

Justice
- Reminder of karma
- Three-fold Law

- What is happening now is a reflection of what you've done in the past
- Whether for good or for bad
- Reminder to act fairly

The Hanged Man

- Being stuck
- In a project, though, or idea
- Sacrifices may have to be made
- The decision must be made to move out of limbo

Death

- A reminder that everything eventually passes Unplanned change
- Endings
- Relationships
- Problems
- New path in life

Temperance

- Reminder to go with the flow of things
- Move with the change, not against it
- Mature love
- Adapting to new situations

The Devil

- Feeling stuck in a bad situation
- Feeling trapped
- Untrustworthy, though charming person

The Tower

- Destruction Danger
- Unexpected setbacks
- Repercussions

The Star

- Hope and faith
- The Universe is encouraging you to have faith Renewal
- Confidence and positivity
- A new life with a broader scope of choice

The Moon

- Intuition Dreams
- Imagination Magical work

The Sun

- Connected to our subconscious
- Possible deception

- Moving in the correct direction
- Happiness
- Vitality and optimism Good news is coming
- Fairly-earned reward

Judgment
- Review of past decisions is needed
- Connects past to future
- A situation is nearing its end

The World
- You are where you're meant to be
- No loose ends
- A good conclusion
- Exploration of new directions

Runes

Runes were also a large part of Witchcraft, known as the first system of writing. They were created by Germanic people and were believed to represent a potent force. Runes are to be used in the traditional way: by carving them into an object. Simply drawing the runes don't hold the same power, as these were very tactile tools since their inception.

The runic alphabets are called futharks, but the first completed alphabet – and the most used – is the Elder Futhark, finished in the year ¢oo. These are extremely powerful tools and should be fully understood before being used.

In divination it's easiest to have these symbols carved into stones or tiles, casting them to the ground and picking three at random. Use the rune's meaning to determine the answer to your question.

The Elder Futhark

Fehu

- Used to advance goals and projects
- Protecting valuables/ property
- Boosting career
- Escalating wealth
- Aiding activity and motivation
- Invoking Fire of Heavenly Bodies
- Greater capacity to receive and send energy

Uruz

- Increases strength
- Removes self-doubt and weakness
- Pulls oak and Earth strength into a personal circle
- Pull in new situations
- Start new processes

- Altering difficulties caused by an abrupt change

Thursaz

- Starts change
- Initiates breakthroughs Brings luck
- Aids protection Stimulate fruitfulness

Ansuz

- Promotes eloquence Increases wisdom
- Heightens spiritual consciousness
- Invokes Divinity within
- Increase inspiration Heighten ecstasy
- Increase psychism Freeing power of Divine
- Remember and cultivate ancestral power Aids in past-life regression

Raidho

- Aids in ritual
- Aids in astral travel Garners justice
- Aids in finding true purpose

- Inaugurate rightful order Draws in good counsel
- Aids in progress
- Attunes cosmic harmonies
- Aids in righting wayward situations
- Removing and redirecting energy
- Aids in divination magic

Kenaz

- Opening rune
- Raises executive ability
- Frees creative impulse
- Unveils secrets
- Discover hidden knowledge
- Aids in love magic
- Lights flame of knowledge
- Heightens cunning
- Unleashes skills
- Heightens artistic skill

Gebo

- Increase balance

- Promotes exchange
- Encourages generosity
- Draws mutual benefit
- Enhances marriage, relationships, and partnerships Aids in bonding
- Brings abundance Aids in luck
- Opens direct line between Divine and human realms

Wunjo

- Rune of wishes
- One of the most powerful in the alphabet
- Heightens harmony with others
- Aids in success Fixes disagreements
- Draws likeminded people
- Heightens empathy
- Aids in friendly interaction and fellowship
- Advocates peace
- Promotes sensuality
- Heightens fruitfulness

Hagalaz

- Protective holism rune
- Wards off evil spells
- Aids shamanic travel between worlds
- Aids in overcoming obstacles
- Removing bad habits
- Helping decision making
- Blessings for partnerships/ marriages

Naudhiz

- Banishment rune
- Frees from constrictions

- Increases ability to turn bad situations good
- War fetter
- Curse binder
- Success in ventures
- Turning frustrations into advantages
- Loosening hold of ill Wyrd
- Karmic destiny

Isa

- Blocking rune
- Stops unwanted activity
- Aids in stillness
- Aids in slowing, hindering, and stopping events
- Provides clarity
- Aids in inward focus
- Heightens concentration and strength
- Weeding out enemies
- Binding
- Stopping harassment Stopping unwanted aggression

Jera

- Draws out gentle revolution
- Aids improvement Promotes change
- Heightens prosperity in peace
- Aids in productive results
- Aids in legal matters Heightens fertility magic
- Aids in luck
- Heightens lasting prosperity

Eihwaz

- Endurance rune
- Aids in achieving goals
- Aids in strengthening self
- Aids in attaining objects
- Heightens ability for survival Protection
- Aids in understanding fate
- Protects against self-destructive behaviors

- Helps find things that are lost
- Aids in finding a job
- Aids in completing difficult tasks

Perthro

- Aids in understanding Wyrd
- Heightens understanding of past incarnations
- Aids in freeing ancestral memories
- Heightens meditation and divination
- Aids in self-hypnosis therapy Answers Earth's mysteries

- Aids in awakening higher consciousness
- Heightens magical power
- Aids in the protection and destruction of danger
- Heightens defense

If one chooses to use runes, it's imperative that one keeps the invocation and meaning in mind, as they can essentially become one of the most powerful tools a Witch has in his/her arsenal.

Scrying

Scrying, also called crystal gazing, is using water in a dark bowl, a dark magic mirror, the flame of a candle, or a crystal ball to divine the future. This could be visual, auditory, emotional, or scent-based.

The point of these items is to occupy your conscious mind, allowing your subconscious to become active.

How to Scry

1. Pick a quiet place to sit with your chosen scrying tool.

2. Relax. Take slow, deep breaths.

3. Let your vision slightly unfocus as you look at your tool.

¢. Do your best to keep your mind clear, as the answers you seek reside within you, not within the tool.

5. Be aware it can take time to understand the answers you're being given.

6. Practice, practice, practice!

You can also use scrying to find someone or something that is lost. By some, this is considered dowsing since you're locating something.

You will need:

A map

A crystal attached to a cord, chain, or string

Steps:

1. Spread out your map on a flat surface.
2. Hold the string on your crystal so it swings back and forth over the map.
3. Focus on your intent: to find (lost keys, a family pet, etc.).
4. Once the crystal has found what you're looking for, you will feel it pull down to the spot on the map.

You can add incense, essential oils, or scented candles to get yourself into an altered state of consciousness that makes it easier to tap into these psychic abilities, just as scent aids us in our magical workings.

It's also helpful to scry at night, as the Moon is the ruler of psychic ability. You may even find it useful to have the Moon Tarot card nearby or another object that symbolizes the Moon.

Water Gazing

This is a simple and inexpensive way to scry.

You can use:

A dark bowl with spring/ distilled water

A regular bowl with water, with a few drops of black ink
A pool

Steps:

1. Choose your tool.
2. Sit with your chosen tool in a quiet space.
3. Clear your mind and take deep breaths.
4. Think about your intent, making sure it's clear.
5. Stare into the water, not hard-focusing.
6. Allow yourself to embrace the knowledge your Divine Self is trying to give to you.

Crystal Gazing

This is arguably the most common form of scrying, as crystals have been used to aid communication for millennia.

Your crystal should:

Only be used for scrying Be clear

Draw you in

Steps:

1. Sit in front of your altar or at a table with your chosen crystal in front of you.

2. Place a candle directly behind your crystal and light it.

3. Breathe deeply until you feel relaxed.

4. Touch your crystal and focus on your intent as you gaze into the crystal.

a. You may wish to see something from a past life, the future, an answer to a question, etc.

5. Feel your energy field linking with that of your crystal.

a. Your goal is to link frequencies with your chosen crystal so that you can use its power to receive information relevant to you.

Fire Gazing

Using a candle's flame may be difficult for beginners, though those with a strong connection to Fire may find this the easiest method. Fire is helpful in tapping into psychic visions.

The same process used in water gazing can be used here.

Mirror Gazing

Black mirrors are great for scrying but can be pricey. Some Witches, particularly those just starting out, choose to make their own black mirrors to save some cash as they practice. You can do this with a cheap mirror and a few coats of black enamel paint.

Mirrors have been used since ancient times for divining purposes and can be very powerful tools in your arsenal.

Steps:

1. Sit in front of your mirror, either so you can see your face, or so you can't.

a. This is simply a preference. Some Witches choose to use their own reflections as an aid in scrying revolving around past-lives, while others find their image distracting, and would rather just work through the glass.

2. Take deep breaths until you feel calm.

3. Soft-focus on your mirror, opening your mind to the knowledge your Higher Self can give you.

Dowsing

Dowsing is a form of divination where a pendulum, metal rod, tuning fork, or even an appropriately shaped tree branch (witch hazel, willow, hazel) is used to answer yes or no questions. Dowsing is usually only used to find objects – whether it be something that's lost, the correct crystal for your next spell, etc.

What you choose to use is up to you, though you should always choose something that resonates with you.

The simplest explanation of dowsing with a tuning fork, metal rod, or tree branch is that you will feel the tool vibrating as it comes in contact with energy. Held lightly in the hand(s) they will turn in the direction of the lost object. As with any magical work, keep your intent clear and focused.

Chapter 8: Essential Oils

What are Essential Oils

Essential oils are a standard piece of magical and ritual practice. They are used to bless crystals, amulets and talismans, ritual tools, and bodies. They can also be used for charm making and candle magic, along with intensifying spell work and rituals.

The scent, as we discussed with incense, is an important part of any magical working, because different smells can allow us to transcend into a different level of consciousness. Several millennia ago, priests, shamans, and healers adopted the practice of using scented oils in medicine, ritual, and magic. Scented oils were used in practically every magical creation imaginable – ointments, tinctures, incense, charms – and were either used singularly or as a blend of two or more.

It is believed that these oils hold the magical energies from the plants they were made from in an intensely concentrated way. This is because plants are an intrinsic part of Nature – living beings.

As we discussed with herbal magic, plants can be used for practically any kind of magic; the same can be said for the essential oils made from them, as they produce a true connection between the spiritual and physical planes.

How to Make Your Owm Essemtial Oils

Thousands of years ago, essential oils were created by warming plant materials like bark, flowers, and leaves, in a carrier oil that was typically made from sesame seeds or olives. Cinnamon, frankincense, and myrrh, very popular oils that are still used today were made using this method.

Now steam distillation and heat presses have been invented, allowing for a larger variety of plats to be used.

Steps to Making Your Own Oils

1. Fill jar 1/3 full of dried herb(s)

2. Pour oil base of choice over herbs to almost full

a. You can use grape seed, jojoba, safflower, olive, apricot, or sesame seed oil

3. Close the lid and gently shake

4. Place in a dark, cool place for 2 to ¢ weeks

5. Every day, twice a day, shake the jar gently

6. Remove lid and put cheesecloth over top, holding with rubber band/ elastic

7. Filter oil by pouring into the second jar, squeeze herbs in cloth to gather the remainder of the oil

8. Use a funnel to pour into small brown or dark blue glass bottles

9. Date and label, then store out of direct sunlight

It's not necessary for you to blend your own essential oils, but it does have its benefits:

More easily acquainted with magical energies associated with the oils

Many inadequate knock-offs exist with the growing popularity of aromatherapy, so mixing your own can assure you they're pure

Steps to Making Your Own Blend

1. Put your carrier oil of choice into a blending jar.

a. The amount depends on the number of essential oil vials one would like to fill

b. The general rule of thumb is 2 tablespoons per set

2. Drop in essential oils one at a time.

3. Mix oils together by swirling them in the jar.

4. Use a funnel to pour the oil into a brown or blue glass bottle.

5. When storing, keep out of direct sunlight.

If you're making your oil for a particular use, visualize your goal while you're making it; this is how you infuse your magical will into your oils.

Where to Buy Essential Oils

Essential oils can be expensive, so only starting with a couple is a great starting place. Not only will it save you money, but it will help keep you from being overwhelmed. Only having a couple of oils to focus on allows you to learn about them without feeling pressured about the possible other 10 that you don't know yet.

These oils can be bought in Wiccan specialty shops, New Age stores, online, and potentially, your local health food store. It's always important to do research beforehand because you don't want to dilute the oils properties by adding ingredients to pure oils. There are certainly reputable places to buy from, even online with a bit of research, and health food shops are typically a safe bet.

Example Oil Blends

Purification Oil
Lavender: 1 drop
Cedarwood: 3 drops
Juniper: 5 drops

Money-Drawing Oil
Lavender: 1 drop
Cypress: 2 drops
Bergamot: 3 drops Patchouli: ¢ drops

Consecration Oil
Cinnamon: 2 drops
Frankincense: 5 drops
Myrrh: 5 drops

Banishing Oil
Cedarwood: 2 drops
Clove: 2 drops
Cypress: 3 drops

Air Element Oil
Neroli: 1 drop
Sandalwood: 3 drops
Lavender: 5 drops

Fire Element Oil

Petiprin: 1 drop

Clove: 1 drop

Rosemary: 2 drops

Ginger: 3 drops

Water Element Oil

Jasmine: 1 drop Ylang Ylang: 2 drops Palmarosa: 3 drops

Earth Element Oil

Cypress: ¢ drops Patchouli: ¢ drops

Energy Oil

Cardamom: 1 drop

Lime: 2 drops Orange: ¢ drops

Fast Action Oil

Cinnamon: 1 drop

Rosemary: 2 drops

Lemon: 2 drops Dragon's blood: 2 drops

Full Moon Oil

Rose: 1 drop

Lemon: 2 drops

Sandalwood: 3 drops

Goddess Oil

Ambergris: 1 drop

Lotus: 1 drop

Lemon: 1 drop

Gardenia: 2 drops

Rose: 3 drops

Healing Oil

Sandalwood: 1 drop

Juniper: 2 drops Rosemary: ¢ drops

Power Oil

Pine: 1 drop

Ginger: 1 drop Orange: ¢ drops

Psychic Oil

Yarrow: 4 drops Lemongrass: 12 drops

Prosperity Oil

Cedarwood: 2 drops

Orange: 3 drops

Patchouli: 3 drops

Protection Oil

Lavender: 1 drop

Frankincense: 2 drops

Rosemary: 3 drops

Spirit Oil

Gardenia: 5 drops

Crocus: 5 drops

Violet: 8 drops

Sandalwood: 8 drops

Sacred Light Oil

Cinnamon: 3 drops

Nutmeg: 3 drops

Sandalwood: 8 drops

House Fresheners/ Cleaners

Using natural cleaners can be both healthier for you and actually help you connect to Nature and the Divine.

Certain air fresheners can even be used in rituals and magical workings in place of incense, making them the perfect solution for those sensitive to smoke. All of these can be made by simply mixing spring water (or distilled water) with the essential oils. You can put them in spray bottles for easy use, so all you have to do is shake them up and let them sit, because the longer they're left alone, the stronger their properties and scents become.

Woodsy Air Freshener

This scent is useful in meditation and good luck, but can also be used to create a space that's sacred for ritual or other magical work.

You will need:

Distilled water: ¢ ounces Cedar essential oil: 20 drops Cypress essential oil: 20 drops

Sandalwood essential oil: 20 drops Pine essential oil: ¢0 drops

Calming Air Freshener

This scent is great for relaxation, whether it be children, adults, or even scared or nervous pets!

You will need:

Distilled water: ¢ ounces Chamomile essential oil: 10 drops Rosemary essential oil: 10 drops Marjoram essential oil: 10 drops Sweet bay essential oil: 10 drops Lavender essential oil: ¢0 drops Sandalwood essential oil: 40 drops

Good Luck into the New Year

This air freshener is great during December, as it's a time to begin preparing for the spring and first harvests, and though it's not considered the end of the year, many modern Wiccans treat December as a time for planning the success and goals of the coming months.

You will need:

Distilled water: ¢ ounces Orange essential oil: 10 drops Clove essential oil: 10 drops Cypress essential oil: 10 drops Allspice essential oil: 10 drops

Eucalyptus essential oil: 10 drops Cedarwood essential oil: 10 drops Cinnamon essential oil: 10 drops Pine essential oil: ¢0 drops

Healing Air Freshener

This scent is great for promoting abundant good health.

You will need:

Distilled water: ¢ ounces Clove essential oil: 10 drops

Sandalwood essential oil: 10 drops Rosemary essential oil: 10 drops Lime essential oil: ¢0 drops Eucalyptus essential oil: ¢0 drops

Prosperity Air Freshener

This air freshener is great for drawing monetary prosperity your way, so can be a good addition to any spellwork or ritual that involves money.

You will need:

Distilled water: ¢ ounces Calendula essential oil: 10 drops Patchouli essential oil: 10 drops Allspice essential oil: 10 drops

Cedar essential oil: 10 drops Bergamot essential oil: 40 drops Peppermint essential oil: 40 drops

Abundant Harvest Air Freshener

This scent is useful during the harvest months and aids in spellwork and rituals pertaining to a prosperous harvest, and ritual work is done on Samhain and Mabon.

You will need:

Distilled water: ¢ ounces Orange essential oil: 10 drops Apple essential oil: 10 drops Dill essential oil: 10 drops Clove essential oil: 10 drops

Cinnamon essential oil: 10 drops Allspice essential oil: 30 drops Ginger essential oil: ¢0 drops

Natural Wood Furniture Polish You will need:

Jojoba carrier oil: 2 ounces Lime essential oil: 5 drops Lemon essential oil: 5 drops

Ylang Ylang essential oil: 10 drops Sealed container

Simply stir all ingredients together and store until needed.

Carpet Freshener 1 You will need:

Clove essential oil: 10 drops Cedar essential oil: 10 drops Patchouli essential oil: 20 drops Lime essential oil: 30 drops Orange essential oil: 30 drops Glass jar with an airtight lid

Steps:

1. Add ingredients to a jar
2. Tightly close the lid and shake vigorously
3. Let sit a minimum of 2¢ hours
4. Light sprinkle on carpet
5. Let sit 15 minutes, then vacuum

Carpet Freshener 2 You will need:

Bicarbonate of soda: ½ cup Eucalyptus essential oil: 10 drops Spruce essential oil: 10 drops Orange essential oil: 20 drops Lavender essential oil: 50 drops Glass jar with an airtight lid

Steps:

1. Add ingredients to a jar
2. Tightly close the lid and shake vigorously
3. Let sit a minimum of 2¢ hours
4. Light sprinkle on carpet
5. Let sit 15 minutes, then vacuum

Chapter 9: Empaths and the Highly In-Tuned

What is am Empath or Highly In-Tuned Persom

Everything in the Universe is made of energy, and that energy emits vibrations. Highly sensitive individuals can be very attuned to the energy of things in Nature, electrical appliances, the energy of the living, or the energy of the dead. Within the grouping of highly sensitive or in-tuned people, are empaths.

Empaths are those who are extremely in-tune with the emotions of others, and if their gift is strong enough, they can even feel other's emotions. Another term for this is 'clairsentient. In those who aren't careful, this can result in the empath taking on those emotions as though they were their own.

How to Determine

If You're am Empath

There are common questions that can help guide you to determine whether or not you have the gift of empathy. If your answer is yes to any of these questions, it's likely you're at least on the scale of highly in-tuned individuals.

Are you able to feel other's emotions? Are people drawn to you?

Do they confide in you easily?

This can include strangers

Do you often know the emotional states of others?

Are you easily emotionally overwhelmed when in crowds? Do you suffer from seemingly random mood swings?

Can you feel the emotions of those you watch on television?

Can you tell if someone is telling the truth or not?

Do you feel drawn to water?

Tips to Manage Being am Empath

Empaths, especially those who aren't aware or haven't practiced controlling their gift, can easily find themselves feeling drained. This is because feeling everyone's emotions can drain your own energy. It causes some empaths to avoid social interaction entirely, closing themselves off from the world around them.

In order to actively participate in the world, there are a few tricks and tips that can enable empaths to live healthy, fulfilled lives, while still using their gift to help others.

Walk in Nature Drink water

In the shower, picture the water washing all the negative energy away

Water is grounding Develop the throat chakra

The throat chakra is the center of personal truth and expression

Opening throat chakra enables empath to express feelings and needs

Singing, meditating, sharing thoughts and feelings, and chanting are helpful in developing throat chakra

Develop the root chakra

The root chakra allows one to feel fully present and grounded and enabling them to be fully present in the world

Opening the root chakra enables empaths to let go of fears that keep them from attaining their highest manifestation

Cleaning and smudging regularly

Smudging yourself ('bathing' in the smoke of specific herbs) clears the energy and influence of others

A bath, shower, or solitude can serve the same purpose

Meditation Shielding

This creates a protective bubble, shielding from the emotions of others and only allowing positive emotions to enter

Enables group activity, being in crowds, etc.

Most choose to envision a white ball of light surrounding them

Essences for Empaths Olive

Yarrow

Beech

Helps soothe those who take on more than a fair share of suffering

Revitalizer

Lightens effects of struggle or fatigue

Remedy for stabilization Energy shield

Aids in shielding extra sensitive individuals who are prone to energies depleting their personal space

Protection from emotional attacks Aids those feeling vulnerable socially

Mountain Pennyroyal

Gives protection Blocks negative energy Gives clarity

Wards off psychic attachments and negativity Aids in purging and cleansing picked up energies

Pink Yarrow

Aids in creating emotional boundaries

Compassion is kept, but without taking their burdens on as own

Dandelion

Cleanses painful memories Removes emotional gunk

Borage

Heather

Fawn Lily

Mallow

Heals heart Lifts burdens

Offers healing and energetic lightness

Aids in determining one's own emotions from collected emotions from others

Aids in recognizing emotions within that don't belong

Aids reclusive individual in rejoining the world Aids in beginning interactions with others

Aids in releasing fear

Aids in the ability to be open

Aids in breaking down self-protective walls

Yellow Star Tulip

Enables those who wish to use their gift as healers Aids in enhancing the natural ability

Heightens ability to identify client's needs Refines knowledge and truth

Manzanita

Helps those who have ignored their human side in favor of their spiritual nature

Aids in embracing one's physical body

Aids in combining the physical and spiritual in order to view the world in a balanced manner

Empaths im the World

It's common for empaths, whether they know they possess this gift or not, to find themselves working as healers – nurses, doctors, counselors, psychologists, etc. They play an important role in the world, though it's not always easy.

If you feel that you're an empath, then the tips above will help you hone your gift – because that's what it is, a gift!

Chapter 10: Popular Terms

Altar: A flat surface used specifically for magical works.

Amulet: An object charged with magical intent, usually for protection, that repels negative energy.

Arcana: Two parts that make up a full Tarot deck.

Astral projection: The psychic process of separating from your physical body in order to travel during dreams or in the astral plane to accomplish your will.

Astral plane: A parallel to our physical world where magical will can be done.

Astrology: The belief and study of how planetary movement affects our lives and behaviors.

Aura: The energy fields that surround every living thing.

Balefire: A magical fire lit outdoors or in the hearth, typically used during Midsummer, Yule, and Beltane.

Banish: To rid oneself of negative energies and influences. Bind: Using magic to restrain someone or something.

Burning times: The historical time when millions of people were killed by the church for suspicion of being the Christian version of Witches.

Call: Invoking the powers of the Divine

Calling the Quarters: Acknowledging the Sacred Elements, Earth, Air, Fire, and Water.

Channeling: A magical process where a spirit is allowed to use the practitioner to communicate.

Charge: A message from the Goddess to all Her children.

Charms: An object that has been imbued with magical energy specific to a task.

Cleansing: Clearing negative energy from a space, an object, or a person.

Cone of Power: Psychic or mystic energy generated by a person or coven for a specific purpose.

Consecrate: To bless a place or object with positive energy, enabling it for magical work.

Covenstead: A place where Witches meet to practice magic, commune with the Divine and each other, and generally feel safe.

Days of Power: Also called Sabbats, and are days when magical workings are especially powerful.

Dedication: The conscious acceptance of the Craft as their chosen path, and the vow to prepare to learn, and study to become adept.

Dosil: Clockwise motion symbolic of positivity and good magic.

Divine Power: The transcendent life force which exists in everything, the energy that the Goddess and God possess.

Drawing Down the Moon: A ritual Witches use to invoke the Goddess and commune with her during the Full Moon.

Duality: The separation of two opposites, seeing them as two separate entities (the God is seen as the Oak King and the Holly King).

Earth Magic: All energy within natural objects that can be used in magical work.

Elementals: The Spirits associated with the Sacred Elements, used when calling upon specific Elements to empower a magical work.

Evoke: To call something from within, out.

Familiar: An animal that is spiritually bound to a Witch.

Gaia: Mother Earth

Grove: Another word for a coven.

Higher Self: That which connects us to the Collective Unconscious, which holds all knowledge of the Universe.

Initiation: Typically, a ritual is welcoming a new member into a coven.

Labrys: Double-headed ax representative of the Goddess' lunar aspect.

Left-Hand Path: Those who practice dark magic to control or harm others.

Macrocosm: Composes the world around us.

Microcosm: Composes the world within us.

New Age: Mixing structured religion with metaphysical practice.

Occult: Hidden metaphysical topics.

Occultist: Someone who practices occult subjects.

Old Ones: All aspects of Goddess and God.

Old Religion/ Old Ways: Alternate name for Paganism.

Pantheon: A collection of Goddesses and Gods specific to a particular mythical or religious structure.

Past-Life Regression: Using meditation to see experiences in one's previous existence.

Polarity: Equal yet opposite energies, much like the God and Goddess.

Projective Hand: Where personal energy leaves the body, the dominant hand.

Receptive Hand: Where energy enters the body, non-dominant hand.

Simple Feast: Dining with the Goddess and God.
Skyclad: Performing magical work nude.

Summerland: Where our life forces go after death.

Widdershins: Counterclockwise motions used to repel negative forces or energies.

Yggdrasil: A symbol for the Tree of Life, which connects all existence.

Conclusion

Thank you for making it through to the end of Wicca Starter Kit: A Complete Beginner's Guide to Wiccan Magic, Spells, Rituals, Essential Oils, and Witchcraft. Let's hope it was informative and able to provide you with all of the tools you need to achieve your goals whatever they may be.

The next step is to begin on your own magical journey! Try out different types of magic – candle, crystal, divination, etc. – and find what you connect with easiest. This is the best way to start practicing and handle the forms more difficult for you once you've gained more experience. Things as simple as growing one or two herbs, placing a few crystals throughout your home, or taking a few minutes of your day to commune with the Goddess and/or the God, can make the transition to Wicca easier than you might expect.

Study as much material as you can get your hands on! This book is a great starting point, but it just scratches the surface of everything there is to know about the Wiccan Path. Find what interests you and start there.

Buy a book on herbalism if you want to hone your green thumb, explore your local Wiccan/ Pagan community to get a sense of communion, look up information on crafting your own spells – whatever first draws your attention is never a bad place to begin learning the Craft.

Remember your Path is as unique as your connection to the Divine. If something doesn't feel right to you, don't do it! Wicca is about your connection to the Source, not the Witch next to you, not the High Priestess – you! Don't be afraid to experiment. Change spells and rituals if they don't work for you, switch ingredients if they don't

speak to you. Your journey is your own, and how you choose to worship the Divine is completely up to you.

Hopefully, the knowledge you obtained here will aid you on the Wiccan Path, serving as a great starting point for your new journey.

Finally, if you found this book useful in any way, a review on Amazon is always appreciated!

Blessed be.

www.ingramcontent.com/pod-product-compliance
Lightning Source LLC
Chambersburg PA
CBHW070106120526
44588CB00032B/1184